Cool Crocheted Hats

Cool Crocheted Hats

40
Contemporary
Designs

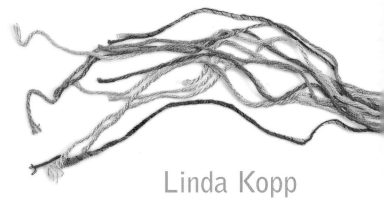

Linda Kopp

LARK BOOKS

A Division of Sterling Publishing Co., Inc.
New York

Art Director: Dana Irwin

Cover Designer: Barbara Zaretsky

Contributing Writers: Terry Taylor

Technical Editor: Karen Manthey

Assistant Art Director: Lance Wille

Art Production Assistant: Jeff Hamilton

Editorial Assistance: Delores Gosnell

Illustrator: Orrin Lundgren

Assistant Editor: Susan Kieffer

Photographer: John Widman

Hair and Makeup: E. Scott Thompson

Library of Congress Cataloging-in-Publication Data

Kopp, Linda, 1960-
  Cool crocheted hats : 40 contemporary designs / Linda Kopp.– 1st ed.
    p. cm.
  Includes index.
  ISBN 1-57990-839-X (hardcover)
  1. Crocheting–Patterns. 2. Hats. I. Title.
TT825.K6938 2006

746.43'40432–dc22

10 9 8 7 6 5 4 3 2 1

First Edition

Published by Lark Books, A Division of
Sterling Publishing Co., Inc.
387 Park Avenue South, New York, N.Y. 10016

Text © 2006, Lark Books
Photography © 2006, Lark Books
Illustrations © 2006, Lark Books

Distributed in Canada by Sterling Publishing,
c/o Canadian Manda Group, 165 Dufferin Street
Toronto, Ontario, Canada M6K 3H6

Distributed in the United Kingdom by GMC Distribution Services,
Castle Place, 166 High Street, Lewes, East Sussex, England BN7 1XU

Distributed in Australia by Capricorn Link (Australia) Pty Ltd.,
P.O. Box 704, Windsor, NSW 2756 Australia

If you have questions or comments about this book, please contact:
Lark Books
67 Broadway
Asheville, NC 28801
(828) 253-0467

Manufactured in China

ISBN 13: 978-1-57990-839-3
ISBN 10: 1-57990-839-X

For information about custom editions, special sales, premium and
corporate purchases, please contact Sterling Special Sales Department
at 800-805-5489 or specialsales@sterlingpub.com.

"Saying you don't look good in a hat is like saying you don't look good in shoes!"
—Unknown

"With the right hat, nothing else matters."
—LaPaloma Hats

"Luxurious, flirty, and, at times, a bit sexy. We're out to prove a great hat can change your day."
—Plaza Suite, New York

"When you wear a hat, it is like medicine for the soul."
—Unknown

CONTENTS

INTRODUCTION

CROCHET BASICS

COOL CROCHETED HATS

STITCHES & TECHNIQUES

APPENDIX

INTRODUCTION

WHETHER IT'S A STYLISH, CLOSE-FITTING CLOCHE, A PLAYFUL PILLBOX, OR A LIDCAP SET AT A RAKISH ANGLE, nothing frames the face and sets the tone of an outfit like a hat. And the good news is that you can create any of these styles and many others with just a few simple crochet stitches.

Never crocheted before? No problem. This book provides you with everything you need to know to make any of the 40 featured hats. The section directly following this introduction explains all the crochet basics you need to know. Included are an overview of the tools, types of yarn, how to read a pattern, and the why and how to make a gauge swatch. At the back of the book you'll find a comprehensive stitch and techniques section that provides instructions for forming all the stitches used in the featured projects, as well as clear step-by-step illustrations. So start with the easy ones—you'll find a wide variety. From the evening-ready Glam Lamé Beanie and the ear-flapped Fuzzy Kitty Hat, to the airy delicacy of the Gatsby Hairpin Lace Cloche, there are incredible hats to suit every occasion and skill level.

If you're an experienced crocheter, skip the basics and head straight for the projects. Whether you're looking for wearable art, updated classics, or today's latest styles, you'll discover contemporary designs sure to inspire you. Lush, rich, texture is highlighted in the Velvet Cabled Beanie, while Partial to Paillettes sparkles with flashy metallic accents. Satisfy your artistic side with Flight of Fancy, a skullie featuring a freeform brooch, or create Julia's Cobalt Blues, a remarkable hat that can be shaped into a multitude of styles. We're delighted to bring you this fabulous collection of hats—the product of a host of talented, creative designers. Whatever your taste, you'll find enough variety to entice you to crochet a different hat every month of the year!

CROCHET BASICS

TOOLS

One of the nice things about crocheting, besides its portability, is how few tools you need to get started—basically just a crochet hook and yarn. There are other tools that are "nice to haves," but are by no means necessary.

HOOKS

The basic design of a crochet hook has remained virtually unchanged since its inception. The tip and throat of the hook are still used to form the stitches, while the diameter of the shaft determines the stitches' size. The grip and handle are used to hold and balance the hook.

If you are just beginning to crochet, aluminum hooks are a good choice because they are lightweight, durable, inexpensive, and easy to hold. There are three different systems of hook sizes. The Continental (European) system uses millimeters, the U.S. (American) uses a combination letter/number system, and the United Kingdom uses a numeric system. Rule of thumb is the higher the letter or number, the larger the hook. And in all cases, the larger the hook, the bigger the resulting stitches.

OTHER TOOLS

Scissors, especially small ones with sharp points, are indispensable. Breaking is not an efficient way to cut yarn. Always use scissors.

Stitch markers are handy when you need to mark the end of a row in your work, the beginning of the round when crocheting in the round, or a specific stitch within a row. If you don't wish to purchase stitch markers, use a coil-less safety pin or a short length of contrasting yarn to mark your spot.

Rulers and flexible tape measures with both standard and metric measurements are useful tools that you probably already have. You will use these tools to measure your work as you progress, and to check your gauge (see page 16).

Rustproof pins of all types—straight pins, T-pins, and safety pins—all have their uses. Make absolutely sure that any type of pin you choose to use is rustproof. Safety pins can be used as stitch markers, and straight pins are great for holding crocheted pieces together as you stitch them.

Tapestry needles (sometimes called yarn needles) with large eyes and blunt points are necessary for finishing a completed crochet project. Using a plastic or metal needle is a matter of preference. Use them to weave loose yarn ends back into your stitches, or to sew together the seams of a hat.

Bags make it easy for you to take your crochet anywhere and everywhere you go. You may choose to tuck your current project, yarn, and a few tools in a plastic grocery bag or invest in a stylish, multipurpose needlework tote. Just be sure your bag doesn't have any tiny holes your hooks or pins might slip through.

WORLD OF YARN

Not long ago, the selection of yarns was, by and large, limited to acrylic, with the most unusual yarns being an occasional cashmere or angora. Happily, yarn shops are now bursting with unique hand-dyed varieties, alpaca to rival the softness of cashmere, downy mohair, crisp linen, and velvety chenille. Exotic fibers from the sheerings of llama, alpaca, buffalo, and musk ox have become quite the rage. Even bamboo and soy are being processed into exquisite yarns. And much to the delight of crocheters everywhere, the offering of novelty yarns has exploded.

TYPES OF YARNS

Yarns are made from animal, plant, and vegetable fibers as well as synthetic fibers, which are from man-made materials. Each fiber has its own strengths and weaknesses, so it stands to reason that a yarn's fiber content is a combination of various fibers in order to capitalize on a fiber's best attributes, and lessen its weaknesses. Following is a brief description of some of the more common yarns you might encounter when making a hat.

Wool has been a popular favorite used throughout the years—and with good cause. Spun from sheep's fleece, it is extremely elastic and durable, and so garments made of wool will hold their shape well and last a good long while. Long appreciated for its warmth, wool is a natural choice for winter wear. An outstanding characteristic of wool is that it can absorb up to one-third of its weight before it actually feels wet, allowing for the gradual absorption and release of perspiration. Wash wool in a woolwash and lay flat to dry. If you like to toss everything in the washer, select a "superwash" wool where the fiber's surface has been coated with a microfine resin. Be mindful not to wash wool in hot water as it may shrink or felt—unless that is your intention.

Alpaca is a member of the camelid family. Yarns spun from alpaca sheerings are soft, lightweight, and extremely strong. The inner core of alpaca fiber is hollow, resulting in a high insulation value for lightweight, yet warm garments. Its incredible softness is often compared to that of the much costlier cashmere yarn, which is made from fiber combed annually from bellies of cashmere goats. Garments made from alpaca yarns should be washed in cool water on the delicate cycle of your washer, or gently hand-washed.

Silk. The silkworm produces long, fine filaments that it uses to spin its cocoon. The filaments are unwound and used to produce a wondrous fiber that absorbs moisture well, and acts as an insulator, keeping you warm in the winter and cool in the summer. Silk fiber is light, yet very strong, and exudes a luxurious luster, making it ideal for creating elegant garments. It is normally combined with other fibers such as wool or cotton, due to its tendency to stretch.

Mohair is spun from the fleece of angora goats and produces a yarn that is valued for its soft, fuzzy appearance. Due to its "hairy" nature, mohair should be used in projects with simple stitches, so as to not obscure more intricate patterns. Many people find mohair to be itchy, so it is wise to combine it with other fibers like alpaca or wool.

Angora fiber is made from the fur of Angora rabbits when they naturally shed their coats or are shorn. The shorn method results in some shorter hairs, and so some shedding may occur. Angora fiber is slippery and so is often blended with wool to increase its workability. Similar to alpaca, the core of angora fibers is hollow, giving the resulting yarn outstanding breathing and wicking capabilities. To clean, machine wash and then dry on a cool cycle.

Cotton yarn is made with the fiber that surrounds the seeds in a cotton pod. We're all familiar with products made from cotton—they absorb moisture, but dry slowly once wet. Items made with cotton are easy to wash, and will hold their shape after washing, although they will start stretching out over time.

Acrylic is a synthetic yarn that boasts several advantages—it's strong, elastic, inexpensive, and is very easy to maintain. Toss it in your washer, pull it out of the dryer, and it's ready to wear again. Acrylic yarns tend to pill (little fuzzy balls that result from fibers rubbing and tangling together), and they don't breathe—meaning they don't wick moisture away from the body. That means if acrylic gets wet, it won't keep you very warm (something you should consider if your intention is to crochet a hat for that purpose).

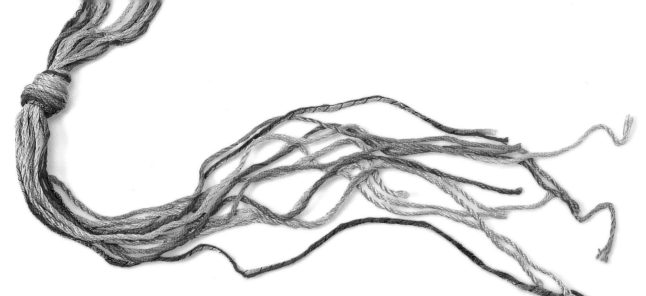

SUBSTITUTING YARNS

Each project in this book gives the particulars of the yarns used, but if a certain color or texture doesn't excite you, then by all means, don't limit yourself to that specific yarn. You may have a yarn in your stash that you envision would be perfect for a particular pattern, or perhaps you have had your eye on a skein and just need a good excuse to buy it. Do it, and substitute! It will only enhance the creative experience and your satisfaction with your finished project.

HOW TO SUBSTITUTE YARNS

The safest route is to always substitute yarns based on the recommended gauge and hook size listed on the label. Bear in mind that it's important that should you choose to substitute yarn besides just for color, be sure to pay close attention to the type of yarn specified in the project, and select yarn of the same weight and size. Otherwise, you may end up with a hat sized for a tot or, conversely, for Paul Bunyan.

Double-check the yardage needed for the project, and make sure you purchase enough of the substitute yarn to equal that amount. To do that, jot down the total length of each ball of the original yarn in the pattern. Multiply the number of balls called for by yards/meters per ball. This will tell you how much yarn you need. Write down the total amount of each yarn type you will need for the project.

Next, when you have found the yarn you wish to use, divide the total yardage you need by the yards/meters per ball of your new yarn, and round up to the next whole number. This will give you the number of skeins you'll need of the substitute yarn.

YARN WEIGHTS AND SIZES

All yarn patterns in this book specify a specific type of yarn. There are six basic categories, based on a yarn's weight or thickness. A yarn's weight refers to it's diameter, or size. You may note that there is some crossover between types. The two terms can be used interchangeably.

Super-Fine weight yarns include fingering, sock, and baby yarns. It is the thinnest yarn type and is used primarily for delicate work like baby clothing and shawls.

Fine weight includes Sport yarns that can be used for a wide variety of projects such as lightweight sweaters, scarves, and ponchos.

Light yarn includes Double Knitting weight yarn (sometimes referred to as DK weight), and is similar to sport weight in that it can be used in the same types of projects, but because it is a bit thicker, it will result in a slightly heavier finished product.

Medium weight yarns include worsted weight, which is one of the most commonly found yarns, widely available at mass merchandisers as well as specialty yarn shops. It is a work-

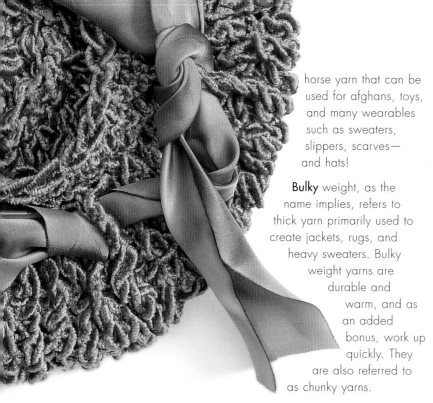

horse yarn that can be used for afghans, toys, and many wearables such as sweaters, slippers, scarves— and hats!

Bulky weight, as the name implies, refers to thick yarn primarily used to create jackets, rugs, and heavy sweaters. Bulky weight yarns are durable and warm, and as an added bonus, work up quickly. They are also referred to as chunky yarns.

Super Bulky is similar to bulky weight in that it is used in the same type of projects, only the yarn is beefier and works up even quicker.

Novelty yarns are attractive, intriguing, and just plain fun! Feast your eyes on vibrant, intricate ladder yarns; finger fringy eyelash and fuzzy, fun furs, and yarns sprouting soft, colorful nubs. These yarns can be used alone or combined with other yarns to add fanciful, trendy accents. Many novelty yarns are easier to work with when used as a "carry-along" yarn, held with a more basic yarn to give it substance. It's best to use plainer yarns for more decorative stitch patterns in order to allow the beauty of the design to show. Save the novelty yarns for trim work and accents, to combine with a plainer yarn, or for simpler patterns.

PATTERN COMPONENTS

The crochet pattern tells you everything you need to know in order to create each hat. Just like a good recipe, everything is spelled out to ensure your success. And just like you were taught to read through a whole recipe first before beginning so there would be no surprises, you should take a few minutes and read the crochet pattern from beginning to end. Consider those minutes as an essential step in the creation process—and a valuable investment of time.

Let's take a moment to look at what the patterns in this book tell you.

EXPERIENCE LEVEL

A pattern indicates which level of experience it's designed for: beginner, easy, intermediate, or experienced.

Beginners will use basic stitches in a straightforward manner. There will be minimal shaping of the project.

Easy patterns use basic stitches, simple repetitive stitch patterns, simple color changes, and easy-to-master shaping and finishing techniques.

Intermediate patterns use a variety of stitches, more complex stitch patterns, and may necessitate complex color changes.

Advanced level patterns will use intricate stitch patterns, work from charted stitches, use finer threads, smaller hooks, and may require finishing.

MATERIALS AND TOOLS

Every pattern will list the materials, the specific hook size, and other tools that you'll need. The pattern will tell you exactly which type of yarn is used and approximately how much you'll need to create the project.

STITCH LIST

The stitches used in the pattern will be listed. If advanced or specialty stitches are used, you'll be given directions for the stitches. These stitches will be listed in abbreviated form to save space (see chart on page 126). If special changes in standard stitch construction or unique working methods are used, those changes will be noted and brought to your attention before you start.

GAUGE

There will be a gauge specified for the design. In order for your project to be the size you want, it is important to make a gauge sample. See page 16 for more information on creating a gauge sample.

Every pattern will be written with step-by-step instructions for every row you crochet. It will begin with the number of chain stitches you need for your foundation row, then continue with a row-by-row description of the stitches or pattern stitches needed to complete the project.

If there are special stitch variations or unusual working methods for the pattern, these will be noted in a separate section of pattern notes or working notes.

If there are specific color changes that make up a pattern for checks or stripes, these changes may be shown graphically with an illustration or a charted graph. Each square on a charted graph will be equal to a given number of stitches.

FINISHING AND ASSEMBLY

Finally, if your project needs to be assembled, the instructions will tell you what to do and, in some cases, how to do it. In addition, if the project calls for embellishments like crocheted flowers or tassels, in most cases you'll be given instructions on how to create them.

TWO KEYS TO SUCCESS:

#1: Read through the directions from beginning to end, row by row, translating each abbreviation into a word or phrase. Then, read the directions aloud. Yes, it sounds like a silly thing to do, but it works.

#2: As you begin to work a specific stitch pattern, make a mantra of the sequence of stitches you need to work. Repeat the mantra to yourself as you make each part of the pattern. After a while, you'll be able to execute the stitch pattern almost without thinking about it.

HOW TO READ A PATTERN

Crochet instructions are written in a special

(but not secret!) language with abbreviations, punctuation marks, and special terms and symbols. They may look mysterious or even foreboding, but with a little practice and a bit of thinking through each direction, you'll soon catch on.

Familiarize yourself with the table of abbreviations on page 126 and refer back to it as often as needed. These standardized abbreviations are commonly used in most crochet instructions around the world. In no time at all, you'll know what hdc means without thinking about it twice.

In addition to abbreviations, you'll need to pay attention to a few special symbols and punctuation marks. They serve a useful purpose when reading crochet directions.

SYMBOLS AND PUNCTUATION

* An asterisk is used to shorten instructions. Work all instructions following an * as many times as indicated.

: A colon tells you to stop and pay attention. Usually a number will follow that tells you the number of stitches you should have in that row or round.

( ) Parentheses are often used to enclose a set of steps and to indicate changes for different sizes.

[ ] Brackets will be used to indicate another block of instructions grouped within parentheses.

GAUGING IMPORTANCE

You pick out an awesome hat pattern, use that fantastic yarn that you've been saving for just the right project, and painstakingly follow each step of the pattern. But to your dismay, your finished hat is two times too large or too small.

So how do you ensure that what you crochet matches the size you want for the project? It's simple: Create a gauge sample each and every time, before you start any project. The gauge of any pattern is stated right after the stitches that are used in the project, right along with hook size and yarn type.

Gauge is measured by stitches, or rows of stitches, per inch. If your project is made solely with single crochet, you'll use single crochet stitches to make the sample. If the project has a set of several different stitches that repeat across the row, you'll need to create a sample for that set of stitches. If you're not very experienced with crochet, you may have a few questions about the process.

WHY SHOULD I MAKE A GAUGE SAMPLE?

It's an excellent way to practice your stitches, and it's the only way to ensure your project will be the size you desire. Every yarn type differs slightly from manufacturer to manufacturer. In the same way, every person who crochets does so a bit differently. Stitch tension varies from person to person and from day to day!

HOW LARGE A SAMPLE DO I NEED TO MAKE?

In general, people tend to crochet tighter at the beginning and end of a row. You'll want to measure your gauge in the sample where the stitches are most consistent—the center. Create a gauge sample that measures 4 x 4 inches or larger. It's imperative that you create your sample with the same yarn and hook that you plan to use to crochet the project.

WHAT DO I DO WITH THE SAMPLE?

For the most accurate measurement of your gauge, you need to treat your sample just as you would your finished project. Lay the sample flat to measure, and count both the number of individual stitches and rows per inch.

WHAT DO I DO IF MY SAMPLE DOESN'T MEASURE UP?

If your sample doesn't result in the specified gauge, do not, I repeat, do not throw up your hands and quit. Simply rework a sample with a larger (or smaller) hook size, or adjust your stitch tension as you crochet until your sample matches the required gauge. It's as simple as that.

COOL CROCHETED HATS
PROJECTS

Simple
CLOCHE

DESIGNER: Lindsay Obermeyer

WORKED IN SPIRALING ROUNDS, this quick-to-make hat has plenty of panache. The decorative buttoned tab is a pleasant accent and makes a nice place to tuck a flower or two.

SKILL LEVEL

Easy

SIZE

This hat is designed to fit most adult heads.

YOU WILL NEED

- 165yd/151m bulky flat ribbon yarn
- Hook: 6.5mm/K-10 1/2 or size needed to obtain gauge
- 2 buttons
- Yarn needle

STITCHES USED

Chain stitch (ch)

Half double crochet (hdc)

Slip stitch (sl st)

GAUGE

First 3 rnds = 2¾" in diameter

12 sts = 4"

8 rows in pattern = 4"

PATTERN NOTES

This hat is worked in spiraling rounds: Do not join rounds. Use a stitch marker to indicate first stitch in round, move it up at beginning of each round. Work stitches of crown (through rnd 13) in back loops (BL) only. Work stitches of brim (rnds 14–17) in front loops (FL) only.

CROWN

Ch 4 and sl st in 1st ch to form ring.

Rnd 1: Ch 1, work 6 sc in ring (6 sc). Do not join, work in a spiral.

Rnd 2: Place marker in 1st st. 2 hdc in ea st around (12 hdc).

Rnd 3: (Hdc in next st, 2 hdc in next st) around (18 hdc).

Rnd 4: 2 hdc in ea st around (36 hdc).

Rnd 5: Hdc in ea st around (36 hdc).

Rnd 6: (Hdc in next 2 sts, 2 hdc in next st) around (48 hdc).

Rnd 7: (Hdc in next 3 sts, 2 hdc in next st) around (60 hdc).

Rnd 8: (Hdc in next 3 sts, 2 hdc in next st) around (70 hdc).

Rnds 9–13: Hdc in ea st around (70 hdc).

BRIM

Work sts in rnds 14–17 in front loops (FL) only.

Rnd 14: Hdc in ea st around (70 hdc).

Rnd 15: (Hdc in next 4 sts, 2 hdc in next st) around (84 hdc).

Rnds 16–17: Hdc in ea st around (84 hdc). At end of last rnd, sl st in next hdc to join. Fasten off. Weave in all yarn ends.

TAB

Ch 15.

Row 1: Working in back loops of sts, work 2 hdc in 2nd ch from hook, hdc in next ch, ch 1, sk next ch (for buttonhole), hdc in each of next 8 ch, ch 1, sk next ch (for buttonhole), hdc in each of last 2 ch. Fasten off. Weave in all yarn ends.

Measure distance between buttonholes on tab. Sew buttons to rnd 12 of crown the same distance apart as buttonholes on tab. Button on the tab.

This project was created with

3 skeins of Crystal Palace's Trio in kiwi-white (#9190), 50% nylon, 50% polyester, 1.75oz/50g = 55yd/50m.

Sunshiny Day
BUCKET

DESIGNER:
Dot Matthews

The puff stitch creates a 3-D effect on this bucket hat. The ultra-soft merino wool results in a relaxed profile and begs to be paired with your favorite sweater and pair of jeans.

SKILL LEVEL

Easy

SIZE

This hat is designed to fit most adult heads.

YOU WILL NEED

- 153yd/138m worsted weight merino wool yarn
- Hook: 6.5mm/K-10 1/2 or size needed to obtain gauge
- Yarn needle

STITCHES USED

Chain stitch (ch)

Single crochet (sc)

Double crochet (dc)

Slip stitch (sl st)

Puff stitch (puff st): (Yo, insert hook in st, yo, draw through st) 4 times in same st (9 loops on hook), yo, draw yarn through 9 loops on hook.

Reverse single crochet (reverse sc): Working from left to right, insert hook in next st to the right, yo, draw yarn through st, yo, draw yarn through 2 loops on hook.

GAUGE

First 3 rnds = 2½" in diameter

12 sts = 4"

14 rows in sc = 4"

PATTERN NOTES

This hat is worked in spiraling rounds through rnd 16: Do not join rounds. Use a stitch marker to indicate first stitch in round, move it up at beginning of each round.

CROWN

Starting at center top, ch 2.

Rnd 1 (right side): Work 12 sc in 2nd ch from hook (12 sc). Do not join, work in a spiral.

Rnd 2: Place marker in 1st st. 2 sc in each sc around (24 sc).

Rnd 3: Sc in each sc around (24 sc).

Rnd 4: *2 sc in next sc, sc in next sc; repeat from * around (36 sc).

Rnd 5: Sc in each sc around (36 sc).

Rnd 6: *2 sc in next sc, sc in each of next 2 sc; repeat from * around (48 sc).

Rnd 7: Sc in each sc around (48 sc).

Rnd 8: *2 sc in next sc, sc in each of next 3 sc; repeat from * around (60 sc).

Rnds 9–15: Ch 1, sc in each sc around (60 sc).

Rnd 16: Ch 1, sc in each sc around (60 sc). Join with sl st in next sc.

Rnd 17: Ch 3 (counts as dc), puff st in next sc, *dc in next sc, puff st in next sc; repeat from * around. Join with sl st in top of ch 3 (30 puff sts).

Rnds 18–19: Ch 1, sc in each st around (60 sc). Join with sl st in 1st sc.

Rnd 20: Ch 1, sc in back loop only of each sc around (60 sc). Join with sl st in 1st sc.

Rnd 21–23: Rep rnds 17–19.

Rnd 24: Rep Rnd 17.

Rnd 25: Ch 1, working from right to left, reverse sc in each st around. Join with sl st in 1st reverse sc. Fasten off. Weave in all yarn ends.

This project was created with

153yd/138m of Malabrigo's Kettle Dyed worsted weight yarn in cadmium, 100% pure merino wool, 3.5oz/100g = 215yd/196m.

JAZZ BERET

DESIGNER: **Lindsay Obermeyer**

SKILL LEVEL

Intermediate

SIZE

This hat is designed to fit most adult heads.

YOU WILL NEED

- Color A: 214 yd/196m of DK weight yarn in black
- Color B: 280 yd/256m of sport weight ribbon in silver
- Hook: 4mm/G-6 or size needed to obtain gauge
- Yarn needle

STITCHES USED

Chain stitch (ch)

Single crochet (sc)

Slip stitch (sl st)

GAUGE

9 sts = 2"

6 rnds sc in back loop only = 1"

THE FRENCH BERET MEETS URBAN CHIC in this hat. It's the perfect fashion accessory for brunch and shopping with the girls, but is equally at home in a sultry jazz club. Ooh-la-la.

PATTERN NOTES

The crown of this hat is worked in rounds in sc worked in back loops only, alternating colored stripes. The hatband is worked in color A only, working in both loops of sts. Hatband covers just the top of the ears. For more coverage, crochet 4 to 6 extra rounds in color A before working trim, following directions for rnds 40–47.

Using color A, ch 5 and sl st in 1st ch to form ring.

CROWN

Work in back loops (BL) only through rnd 30, alternating color A and color B.

Rnd 1: Ch 1, work 10 sc in ring. Join with sl st in 1st sc (10 sc). Fasten off A, join color B. Work all odd-numbered rnds of crown with color A. Carry yarn on wrong side of work to be picked up in later rnd.

Rnd 2: With color B, ch 1, 2 sc in ea sc around. Join with sl st in 1st sc (20 sc). Fasten off color B, pick up color A. Work all even numbered rnds of crown with color B. Carry yarn on wrong side of work to be picked up in later rnd.

Work in the following color sequence throughout crown: *1 rnd color A; 1 rnd color B. Repeat from * through rnd 30. Carry colors on wrong side to be picked up in later rnd.

Rnd 3: Ch 1, sc in ea sc around. Join with sl st in 1st sc (20 sc).

Rnd 4: Ch 1, 2 sc in ea sc around. Join with sl st in 1st sc (40 sc).

Rnd 5: Ch 1, sc in ea sc around. Join with sl st in 1st sc (40 sc).

Rnd 6: Ch 1, (sc in sc, 2 sc in next sc) around. Join with sl st in 1st sc (60 sc).

Rnd 7: Ch 1, sc in ea sc around. Join with sl st in 1st sc (60 sc).

Rnd 8: Ch 1, (sc in next 14 sc, 2 sc in next sc) around. Join with sl st in 1st sc (64 sc).

Rnd 9: Ch 1, sc in ea sc around. Join with sl st in 1st sc (64 sc).

Rnd 10: Rep rnd 6 (96 sc).

Rnds 11–19: Ch 1, sc in ea sc around. Join with sl st in 1st sc (96 sc).

Rnd 20: Rep rnd 6 (144 sc).

Rnds 21–27: Ch 1, sc in ea sc around. Join with sl st in 1st sc (144 sc).

Rnd 28: Ch 1, (sc in next 2 sc, 2 sc in next sc) around. Join with sl st in 1st sc (192 sc).

Rnds 29–30: Ch 1, sc in ea sc around. Join with sl st in 1st sc (192 sc).

Work in color A only, working in back loops (BL) only of sts through rnd 39.

Rnd 31: Ch 1, sc in ea sc around. Join with sl st in 1st sc (192 sc).

Rnd 32: Ch 1, (sc in next 3 sc, skip next sc) around. Join with sl st in 1st sc (144 sc).

Rnd 33: Ch 1, (sc in next 3 sc, skip next sc) around. Join with sl st in 1st sc (108 sc).

Rnds 34–35: Ch 1, sc in ea sc around. Join with sl st in 1st sc (108 sc).

Rnd 36: Ch 1, (sc in next 5 sc, skip next sc) around. Join with sl st in 1st sc (90 sc).

Rnds 37–39: Ch 1, sc in ea sc around. Join with sl st in 1st sc (90 sc).

HATBAND

Work in color A only, working in both loops of sts through rnd 47.

Rnds 40–47: ch 1, sc in each sc around. Join with sl st in 1st sc (90 sc). Fasten off. Weave in all ends.

TRIM

With RS facing, join color B in any sc, working in both loops of sts, *ch 3, 1 sl st in 3rd ch from hook (for picot), sk next sc, 1 sl st in next sc. Repeat from * around. Fasten off. Weave in all ends.

This project was created with

2 balls of Jo Sharp's Classic DK Wool in black (#302), 100% wool, 1.75oz/50g = 107yd/98m. 1 ball of Katia's Granada in silver (#7), 64% nylon/36% polyester, 1.75oz/50g = 140yd/128m.

Bold Contrast
Square Hat

DESIGNER:
Kalpna Kapoor

THIS DISTINCTIVE HAT REQUIRES CONFIDENCE to wear, and is sure to invite compliments. Wear it with attitude! It's a great hat for the beginner crocheter.

SKILL LEVEL

Beginner

SIZE

This hat is designed to fit most adult heads.

YOU WILL NEED

- Color A: 143yd/131m chunky weight yarn in black
- Color B: 143yd/131m chunky weight yarn in white
- Hook: 5.5mm/I-9 or size to obtain gauge
- Yarn needle

STITCHES USED

Chain stitch (ch)

Half double crochet (hdc)

GAUGE

Take time to check your gauge.

12 sts = 4" in pattern.

10 rows = 4" in hdc.

PATTERN NOTES

This hat is worked flat in one piece in a 2-row stripe pattern. Scarf is then folded in half and joined across sides. To change color: Work last hdc of 1st color until 3 loops are on hook, with 2nd color, yo, draw through 3 loops on hook. Drop 1st color and carry up side to be picked up in later row.

Starting at bottom edge, with color A, ch 30 + 2 (counts as 1st hdc).

Row 1: Hdc in 3rd ch from hook, hdc in each ch across (31 hdc). Ch 2, turn.

Row 2: Hdc in each st across (31 hdc). Complete last st with color B, drop color A to be picked up later. With B, ch 2, turn.

Rows 3–34: Rep Row 2, working in the following color sequence: *2 rows color B, 2 rows color A; repeat from * throughout. Fasten off. Weave in all yarn ends.

ASSEMBLY

With RS facing, fold piece in half matching sts across sides. Using yarn needle and matching colors, matching sts across sides, sew side seams.

TASSELS

Cut nine 11" lengths of colors A and B. Weave bundle of color A strands through one top corner of hat. Draw ends even, tie a separate strand of color A, several times around folded bundle approximately 1 inch below folded end of tassel. Tie strand in a knot to secure. Trim ends even. Using color B, repeat tassel on other top corner of hat.

This project was created with

1 ball each of Plymouth Yarn's Encore Chunky in black (#217) (color A) and white (#208) (color B), 75% acrylic/25% wool, 3.5oz/100g = 143yd/131m.

Widow's Peak Hat

DESIGNER:

Hollie Dzama

WHAT MORE COULD YOU ASK FROM A HAT than to be wonderfully colorful, extremely soft, and delightfully nubby? How about tasseled earflaps and a defining widow's peak? Now that's nirvana.

SKILL LEVEL

Easy

SIZE

This hat will fit most adult heads.

YOU WILL NEED

- Approx 152yd/139m thick & thin chunky weight wool yarn in pastels
- Hook: 6.5mm/K-10 1/2 or size needed to obtain gauge
- Yarn needle

STITCHES USED

Chain st (ch)

Single crochet (sc)

Slip stitch (sl st)

Sc2tog (single crochet decrease): Insert hook into st and draw up a loop, insert hook in next st and draw up a loop, yo, draw through all loops on hook.

GAUGE

Take time to check your gauge.

10 sts and 13 rows = 4" in sc in back loop only

PATTERN NOTES

This hat is worked from the bottom up in spiraling rounds; do not join rounds unless otherwise stated. Use a stitch marker to indicate first stitch in round, move it up at beginning of each round. The earflaps and widow's peak will be crocheted in rows. Stitches are worked in back loop only throughout.

CROWN

Starting at bottom edge, ch 54 (or desired length to fit around head) and without twisting ch, sl st in 1st ch to form ring.

Rnd 1 (right side): Ch 1, working in bottom loop of ch, sc in each ch around (54 sc). Do not join, work in a spiral.

Rnd 2: Place marker in 1st st, working in back loops of sts, sc in each sc around (54 sc).

Rnds 3–13: Rep Rnd 2 for 11 more rnds or until hat measures 3½" from beginning.

Rnd 14: Working in back loops only, *sc in each of next 16 sc, sc2tog in the next 2 sc; repeat from * around (51 sts).

Rnd 15: Working in back loops only, *sc in each of next 15 sc, sc2tog in the next 2 sc; repeat from * around (48 sts).

Rnd 16: Working in back loops only, *sc in each of next 6 sc, sc2tog in the next 2 sc; repeat from * around (42 sts).

Rnd 17: Working in back loops only, *sc in each of next 5 sc, sc2tog in the next 2 sc; repeat from * around (36 sts).

Rnd 18: Working in back loops only, *sc in each of next 4 sc, sc2tog in the next 2 sc; repeat from * around (30 sts).

Rnd 19: Working in back loops only, *sc in each of next 3 sc, sc2tog in the next 2 sc; repeat from * around (24 sts).

Rnd 20: Working in back loops only, *sc in each of next 2 sc, sc2tog in the next 2 sc; repeat from * around (18 sts).

Rnd 21: Working in back loops only, *sc in next sc, sc2tog in the next 2 sc; repeat from * around (12 sts).

Rnd 22: Working in back loops only, *sc2tog in the next 2 sc; repeat from * around. Join with sl st in next sc (6 sts). Fasten off, leaving a sewing length. Weave sewing length through sts in last rnd. Draw tight and secure. Weave in all yarn ends.

WIDOW'S PEAK

Work now progresses in rows.

Row 1: With RS facing, working on opposite side of foundation ch, join yarn in any ch to work across front of hat, ch 1, sc in same ch, sc in each of next 9 ch. Ch 1, turn leaving remaining sts unworked (10 sc).

Row 2: Ch 1, working in back loops of sts, sc2tog in 1st 2 sts, sc in each sc across to last 2 sts, sc2tog in last 2 sts. Ch 1, turn (8 sts).

Rows 3–4: Repeat row 2 (4 sts at end of last row).

Row 5: Ch 1, working in back loops of sts, (sc2tog in next 2 sc) twice. Ch 1, turn (2 sts).

Row 6: Ch 1, working in back loops of sts, sc2tog in next 2 sts (1 st). Fasten off. Weave in all yarn ends.

FIRST EARFLAP

Row 1: With RS facing, working on opposite side of foundation ch, skip 4 sts to the left of last st made in Row 1 of widow's peak, join yarn in next ch, ch 1, sc in same ch, sc in each of next 11 ch. Ch 1, turn leaving remaining sts unworked (12 sc).

Row 2: Ch 1, working in back loops of sts, sc2tog in 1st 2 sts, sc in each sc across to last 2 sts, sc2tog in last 2 sts. Ch 1, turn (10 sts).

Rows 3–5: Repeat row 2 (4 sts at end of last row).

Row 6: Ch 1, working in back loops of sts, (sc2tog in next 2 sc) twice. Ch 1, turn (2 sts).

Row 7: Ch 1, working in back loops of sts, sc2tog in next 2 sts (1 st). Fasten off. Weave in all yarn ends.

SECOND EARFLAP

Row 1: With RS facing, working on opposite side of foundation ch, skip 12 sts to the left of last st made in Row 1 of first earflap, join yarn in next ch, ch 1, sc in same ch, sc in each of next 11 ch. Ch 1, turn leaving remaining sts unworked (12 sc).

Rows 2–7: Rep rows 2–7 of first earflap. Weave in all yarn ends.

TIES

Attach three 16" lengths of yarn on tip of one earflap. Braid 3 strands together. Tie in an overhand knot. Repeat on other earflap.

This project was created with

Approx 152yd/139m thick & thin chunky weight wool yarn in pastels.

Textured

LIRS BERET

DESIGNER:

Jonathan James

Texture, texture, and more texture—this freeform hat is loaded with it! You can create this beret using partial balls of your favorite yarns. This design includes a bit of chenille for sheer comfort, a smidgen of nubby yarn for dimension, and a touch of fun fur—well for fun, of course.

SKILL LEVEL

Easy

SIZE

This hat will fit most adult heads.

YOU WILL NEED

- Color A: 1 skein of worsted weight homespun yarn in forest green
- Color B: 1 skein of worsted weight chenille yarn in mauve
- Color C: 1 skein of feather/fun fur type yarn in burgundy
- Color D: 1 skein of bulky/nubby type yarn in multi-colors, primarily blue and purple
- Yarn needle
- Hooks: 4mm/ G-6 and 5mm/H-8 or sizes needed to obtain gauge.

STITCHES USED

Chain stitch (ch)

Single crochet (sc)

Front post single crochet (fpsc): Insert hook from front to back to front again, around the post of the next st, yo, draw through st, yo, draw through 2 loops on hook.

Double crochet (dc)

Slip stitch (sl st)

GAUGE

Take time to check your gauge.

Gauge may vary depending on yarn and hook used. As a guide, use yarns and hooks that will achieve the following gauges:

With H-8 hook and A, first 3 rnds = 2" in diameter; 16 sts = 4"

PATTERN NOTES

This hat is worked in rounds from the top down. Rnd 6 is marked for later addition of a flap. Rnds 15–25 form a second flap. Rnd 14 is marked for later addition of sides, worked on wrong side of hat.

CROWN

With color A and H-8 hook, ch 4, sl st in 1st ch to form ring.

Rnd 1: Ch 1, work 8 sc in ring. Join with sl st in 1st sc (8 sc).

Rnd 2: Ch 1, 2 sc in each sc around. Join with sl st in 1st sc (16 sc).

Rnd 3: Ch 1, sc in each sc around. Join with sl st in 1st sc (16 sc).

Rnd 4: Ch 1, 2 sc in each sc around. Join with sl st in 1st sc (32 sc).

Rnd 5: Ch 1, *sc in next 7 sc, 2 sc in next sc; repeat from * around. Join with sl st in 1st sc (36 sc).

Rnd 6: Ch 1, sc in back loop of each sc around. Join with sl st in 1st sc (36 sc). Mark rnd for placement of top flap.

Rnd 7: Repeat rnd 4 (72 sc).

Rnd 8: Ch 1, sc in each sc around. Join with sl st in 1st sc (72 sc).

Rnd 9: Ch 5 (counts as dc, ch 2), sk next 2 sc, *dc in next sc, ch 2, sk next 2 sc; repeat from * around. Join with sl st in 3rd ch of ch 5 (24 ch-2 spaces).

Rnd 10: Ch 1, 3 sc in each ch-2 space around. Join with sl st in 1st sc (72 sc).

Rnd 11: Ch 1, *sc in each of next 17 sc, 2 sc in next sc; repeat from * around. Join with sl st in 1st sc (76 sc).

Rnd 12: Ch 1, *sc in each of next 18 sc, 2 sc in next sc; repeat from * around. Join with sl st in 1st sc (80 sc).

Rnd 13: Ch 1, *sc in each of next 19 sc, 2 sc in next sc; repeat from * around. Join with sl st in 1st sc (84 sc).

Rnd 14: Ch 1, *sc in sc, ch 1, sk next sc; repeat from * around. Join with sl st in 1st sc (42 ch-1 spaces). Mark rnd for placement of sides.

OUTER FLAP

Rnd 15: Ch 1, work 2 sc in each ch-1 space around. Join with sl st in 1st sc (84 sc).

Rnds 16–17: Ch 1, sc in each sc around. Join with sl st in 1st sc (84 sc). Fasten off A, join color D.

Rnd 18: With D, ch 1, *sc in each of next 13 sc, 2 sc in next sc; repeat from * around. Join with sl st in 1st sc (92 sc).

Rnd 19: Ch 1, *sc in each of next 22 sc, 2 sc in next sc; repeat from * around. Join with sl st in 1st sc (96 sc).

Rnd 20: Ch 1, *sc in each of next 23 sc, 2 sc in next sc; repeat from * around. Join with sl st in 1st sc (100 sc).

Rnd 21: Ch 1, *sc in each of next 24 sc, 2 sc in next sc; repeat from * around. Join with sl st in 1st sc (104 sc).

Rnd 22: Ch 1, *sc in each of next 23 sc, 2 sc in next sc; repeat from * around. Join with sl st in 1st sc (108 sc).

Rnds 23–25: Ch 1, sc in each sc around. Join with sl st in 1st sc (108 sc). Fasten off.

SIDES

Rnd 1: With WS facing, join color A around the post of any sc in marked rnd 14, ch 1, (fpsc, ch 1) around the post of each sc around. Join with sl st in 1st sc (42 ch-1 spaces).

Rnd 2: Ch 3 (counts as dc), dc in each sc and each ch-1 space around. Join with sl st in 1st sc (84 dc).

Rnds 3–4: Ch 1, sc in each st around. Join with sl st in 1st sc (84 sc).

Rnd 5: Ch 1, *sc in sc, ch 1, sk next sc; repeat from * around. Join with sl st in 1st sc (42 ch-1 spaces).

Rnd 6: Ch 1, (sc, ch 1) in each ch-1 space around. Join with sl st in 1st sc (42 ch-1 spaces). Fasten off A, join color B.

Rnd 7: With B, sc in each sc and each ch-1 space around. Join with sl st in 1st sc (84 sc).

Rnd 8: Ch 1, sc in each sc around. Join with sl st in 1st sc (84 sc). Fasten off B, join color C.

Rnd 9: With G-6 hook and C, ch 1, sc in each sc around. Join with sl st in 1st sc (84 sc). Fasten off.

TOP FLAP

Rnd 1: With RS facing, join color B in remaining lp of any sc in Rnd 5, ch 1, working in remaining lps of sts, sc in each sc around. Join with sl st in 1st sc (36 sc).

Rnd 2: Ch 1, sc in each sc around. Join with sl st in 1st sc. (36 sc). Fasten off B, join color C.

Rnd 3: With G-6 hook and C, ch 1, sc in each sc around. Join with sl st in 1st sc (36 sc). Fasten off. Weave in all yarn ends.

This project was created with

1 skein of worsted weight homespun yarn in forest green (color A)

1 skein of worsted weight chenille yarn in mauve (color B)

1 skein of feather/fun-fur type yarn in burgundy (color C)

1 skein of bulky/nubby type yarn in multi-colors, primarily blue and purple (color D)

Ribbed Mohair
PAGEBOY

DESIGNER: Jennifer Hansen

PAGEBOY, NEWSBOY, CABBIE CAP—call it what you like, the look is fun and fabulous. Working two pieces, then crocheting them together around a plastic form cut from a water jug, creates the brim.

SKILL LEVEL

Intermediate

SIZE

This hat is designed to fit most adult heads.

YOU WILL NEED

- 330yd/302m mohair blend yarn
- 1yd/.9m 1½" satin silk ribbon
- Clean plastic milk or water jug
- Hook: 6.5mm/K or size needed to obtain gauge

STITCHES USED

Chain stitch (ch)

Double crochet (dc)

Reverse Single Crochet (rsc)

Single Crochet (sc)

Slip stitch (sl st)

Sc2tog (single crochet decrease) Insert hook in next st and draw up a loop, insert hook in next st and draw up a loop, yo, draw through all loops on hook.

Dc2tog (double crochet decrease): Yo, insert hook in next st and draw up a loop, yo and draw through 2 loops, yo, insert hook in next st and draw up a loop, yo, draw through 2 loops, yo, draw through all loops on hook.

GAUGE

Take time to check your gauge.

1 sts and 16 rows = 4" in sc

9 sts = 4" in body pattern

8 rows = 3½" in body pattern

PATTERN NOTES

This beanie is worked from the top down in rounds without turning. The brim is created by working 2 pieces, then crocheting them together around a plastic form cut from a milk or water jug.

CROWN

Magic Ring: Wrap yarn twice around finger, insert hook in resulting ring, yo, draw yarn through ring, ch 1 to secure.

Rnd 1: Ch 3 (counts as dc), Work 9 dc in ring. Use tail of ring to tighten loosely, but leave enough room for hook to pass. Join with sl st in top of ch 3 (10 dc).

Rnd 2: Ch 1, working from left to right, rsc in same st, rsc in front loop of each st around. Join with sl st in first st (10 rsc).

Rnd 3: Sl st in back loop of 1st st in Rnd 1, ch 3 (counts as dc), working in remaining loops of sts in Rnd 1, dc in 1st st, 2 dc in back loop of each dc around. Join with a sl st in top of ch 3 (20 dc).

Rnd 4: Rep Rnd 2 (20 rsc).

Rnd 5: Sl st in back loop of 1st st in Rnd 3, ch 3 (counts as dc), working in back loops of sts in Rnd 3, dc in 1st st, dc in next dc, *2 dc in next dc, dc in next dc; rep from * around. Join with a sl st in top of ch 3 (30 dc).

Rnd 6: Rep Rnd 2 (30 rsc).

Rnd 7: Sl st in back loop of 1st st in Rnd 5, ch 3 (counts as dc), working in back loops of sts in Rnd 5, dc in 1st st, dc in each of next 2 dc, *2 dc in next dc, dc in each of next 2 dc; rep from * around. Join with a sl st in top of ch 3 (40 dc).

Rnd 8: Rep Rnd 2 (40 rsc).

Rnd 9: Sl st in back loop of 1st st in Rnd 7, ch 3 (counts as dc), working in back loops of sts in Rnd 7, dc in 1st st, dc in each of next 3 dc, *2 dc in next dc, dc in each of next 3 dc; rep from * around. Join with a sl st in top of ch 3 (50 dc).

Rnd 10: Rep Rnd 2 (50 rsc).

Rnd 11: Sl st in back loop of 1st st in Rnd 9, ch 3 (counts as dc), working in back loops of sts in Rnd 9, dc in 1st st, dc in each of next 4 dc, *2 dc in next dc, dc in each of next 4 dc; rep from * around. Join with a sl st in top of ch 3 (60 dc).

Rnd 12: Rep Rnd 2 (60 rsc).

Rnd 13: Sl st in back loop of 1st st in Rnd 11, ch 3 (counts as dc), working in back loops of sts in Rnd 11, dc in 1st st, dc in each of next 5 dc, *2 dc in next dc, dc in each of next 5 dc; rep from * around. Join with a sl st in top of ch 3 (70 dc).

Rnd 14: Rep Rnd 2 (70 rsc).

Rnd 15: Sl st in back loop of 1st st in Rnd 13, ch 3 (counts as dc), working in back loops of sts in Rnd 13, dc in 1st st, dc in each of next 6 dc, *2 dc in next dc, dc in each of next 6 dc; rep from * around. Join with a sl st in top of ch 3 (80 sts).

Rnd 16: Rep Rnd 2 (80 rsc).

Rnd 17: Sl st in back loop of 1st st in Rnd 15, ch 3 (counts as dc), working in back loops of sts in Rnd 15, *dc2tog in next 2 sts, dc in each of next 6 dc; rep from * around. Join with a sl st in top of ch 3 (70 sts).

Rnd 18: Rep Rnd 2 (70 rsc).

Rnd 19: Sl st in back loop of 1st st in Rnd 17, ch 3 (counts as dc), working in back loops of sts in Rnd 17, *dc2tog in next 2 sts, dc in each of next 5 dc; rep from * around. Join with a sl st in top of ch 3 (60 sts).

Rnd 20: Rep Rnd 2 (60 rsc).

Rnd 21: Sl st in back loop of 1st st in Rnd 19, ch 3 (counts as dc), working in back loops of sts in Rnd 19, *dc2tog in next 2 sts, dc in each of next 4 dc; rep from * around. Join with a sl st in top of ch 3 (50 sts).

Rnd 22: Rep Rnd 2 (50 rsc).

Rnd 23: Sl st in back loop of 1st st in Rnd 21, ch 3 (counts as dc), working in back loops of sts in Rnd 21, *dc2tog in next 2 sts, dc in each of next 3 dc; rep from * around. Join with a sl st in top of ch 3 (40 sts).

Fit the hat to wearer's head and if smaller size is required, decrease required number of stitches evenly around next rnd.

Rnd 24: Ch 1, working in both loops of sts, sc in each st around, working sc2tog to decrease as many times as needed to achieve desired fit. Join with a sl st in first st.

Rnd 25: Ch 1, sc in each st around. Join with sl st in first sc. Fasten off.

BRIM

(Make 2)

Starting at front edge, ch 10.

Row 1 (right side): Sc in 2nd ch from hook, sc in each ch across. Ch 1, turn (9 sc).

Row 2: 2 sc in each of 1st 2 sc, sc in each of next 6 sc, 2 sc in each of last 2 sc. Ch 1, turn (13 sc).

Row 3: 2 sc in the 1st sc, sc in each sc across to last sc, 2 sc in last sc. Ch 1, turn (15 sc).

Rows 4–6: Rep Row 3 (21 sc at end of last row).

Row 7: Sc in each sc across. Ch 1, turn (21 sts).

Row 8: Rep Row 3 (23 sc).

LEFT SIDE

Row 9: Sc in each of next 9 sc. Do not ch 1, turn leaving remaining sts unworked (9 sc).

Row 10: Sk first st, sc2tog in next 2 sts, sc in each sc across. Ch 1, turn (7 sts).

Row 11: Sc in each of 1st 5 sc. Ch 1, turn leaving remaining sts unworked (5 sts).

Row 12: Sc2tog in 1st 2 sts, sc in each of next 2 sc, 2 sc in last sc. Ch 1, turn (5 sts).

Row 13: Sc in each of 1st 4 sc. Ch 1, turn leaving remaining st unworked (4 sts).

Row 14: Sc2tog in 1st 2 sts, sc in each of next 2 sc. Ch 1, turn (3 sts).

Row 15: Sc in each of 1st 2 sts. Ch 1, turn leaving remaining st unworked (2 sc).

Row 16: Sc2tog in 1st 2 sts. Ch 1, turn (1 st).

Row 17: Sc in sc (1 sc). Fasten off.

RIGHT SIDE

Row 9: With RS facing, skip 4 sc to the left of last st made in Row 9 of left side, join yarn in next sc, ch 1, skip 1st st, sc in each sc across. Ch 1, turn (9 sc).

Row 10: Sc in each of 1st 7 sc. Do not ch 1, turn leaving remaining sts unworked (7 sts).

Row 11: Sk first st, sc2tog in next 2 sts, sc in each sc across. Ch 1, turn (5 sts).

Row 12: 2 sc in 1st sc, sc in each of next 3 sc. Ch 1, turn leaving remaining st unworked (5 sts).

Row 13: Sc2tog in 1st 2 sts, sc in each of next 3 sc. Ch 1, turn (4 sts).

Row 14: Sc in each of 1st 3 sts. Ch 1, turn leaving remaining st unworked (3 sc).

Row 15: Sc2tog in 1st 2 sts, sc in next sc. Ch 1, turn (2 sts).

Row 16: Sc2tog in 1st 2 sts. Ch 1, turn. (1 st).

Row 17: Sc in sc (1 sc). Fasten off.

FINISHING

Weave in all yarn ends. With WS facing, place 2 Brims together, matching sts. Join yarn in row-end st at end of last row of right side, ch 1, working through double thickness, sc evenly rounded outer edge of brims to last row of left side. Fasten off, leaving a tail that is 3 times the length of the edge of brim that will attach to hat. Cut flat piece of plastic from a clean gallon milk jug or water container to the shape of the brim and insert between the upper and lower brim parts. Fit hat to wearer's head, and hold up brim to desired attachment

point. Mark brim attachment points on hat edge with safety pins. Note: The hat fabric will need to be stretched to fit to brim during sewing of brim to hat. Sew brim to hat through both upper and lower brim to securely enclose plastic brim stiffener.

Weave ribbon through openings in fabric between sts in Rnd 23 as pictured. Tie ends of ribbon in a knot on inside of hat. Cut excess ribbon.

This project was created with

2 balls of Fiesta Yarns La Boheme in Poppies (#11214), 50% rayon/14%wool/4% Nylon/32% Brushed Kid Mohair, 4oz/113g = approx 165yd/151m

1yd Hanah Silk 1½" satin silk ribbon in Hot Flash (HF)

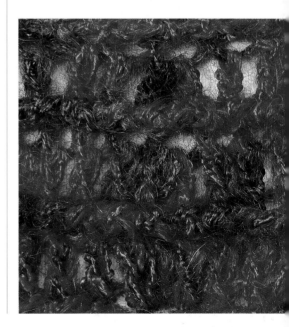

Houndstooth LIDCAP

DESIGNER: Don Halstead

We like this lidcap's flat top and slightly hourglass shape. Not only is it simple to experiment with color combinations using the two-color houndstooth pattern, but the pattern can also be easily altered to fit a child.

SKILL LEVEL

Advanced

SIZE

This hat is designed to fit most adult heads.

FINISHED MEASUREMENTS

Hat: 20½" circumference

YOU WILL NEED

Version 1:

- Color A: 40yd/37m sport weight cotton yarn in black
- Color B: 40yd/37m sport weight cotton yarn in turquoise

Version 2:

- Color A: 40yd/37m sport weight cotton yarn in black
- Color B: 40yd/37m sport weight cotton yarn in white
- Hook: 4mm/G-6 or size needed to obtain gauge

STITCHES USED

Chain stitch (ch)

Single crochet (sc)

Slip stitch (sl st)

GAUGE

Take time to check your gauge

9 sts and 9 rows = 2" in sc

First 3 rnds of top = 2" in diameter

PATTERN NOTES

Pattern creates an hourglass-shaped flat-topped lidcap. Because of the two-color technique involved, cap will not stretch as much as a typical crocheted piece. Hat should fit somewhat tightly to head for the hourglass shape to be created in body of the cap. You can experiment with color alternatives as this design was created to work very easily with just about any color combination you may choose. Substituting materials (for example, wool rather than cotton) should be tested for sizing and appearance.

The color pattern can easily be adjusted by adding or subtracting multiples of 4 stitches. Always crochet a test swatch first to achieve gauge, and it is advised you try on Lidcap after about 4 rounds are crocheted to make sure it fits properly. If you need to increase or decrease size of cap, increase or decrease the foundation ch in increments of 4 stitches to accommodate the charted pattern.

Sides are worked in two colors following a chart for color changes. Read all rows from right to left, repeating from A to B around. To change color, work last sc of first color until 2 loops remain on hook, yo with second color, draw yarn through 2 loops on hook, drop first color, and carry loosely across to be picked up later, work over first color with second color. Sides can be worked to any depth

you would like. Directions are for a hat that is 3½" deep.

Top is worked in back loop only throughout, in spiraling rounds; do not join rounds unless otherwise stated. Use a stitch marker to indicate first stitch in round, move it up at beginning of each round.

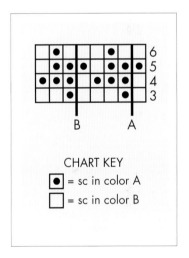

CHART KEY

⊡ = sc in color A

☐ = sc in color B

SIDES

Starting at bottom edge, with color A, ch 92 (or a multiple 4 ch sts to fit snugly around top of head) and without twisting ch, sl st in 1st ch to form ring.

Rnd 1 (right side): Ch 1, sc in each ch around. Join with sl st in 1st sc (92 sc).

Rnd 2: Ch 1, sc in each sc around. Join with sl st in 1st sc (92 sc).

Rnd 3: With color A, ch 1, *with A, sc in sc, drop A, join B, with B, sc in

each of next 3 sc, drop B, pick up A; rep from * around (1st row of chart complete). Join with sl st in 1st sc (23 pattern repeats; 92 sc).

Rnds 4–6: Work even in sc following chart for color changes, reading all rows from right to left; repeat from A to B around. Join with sl st in 1st sc (23 pattern repeats; 92 sc).

Rows 7–14: Repeat rows 3–6 twice.

Rows 15–16: Repeat rows 3–4.

TOP

With color A, ch 3 and sl st in 1st ch to form ring.

Rnd 1 (right side): Ch 1, 2 sc in back loop of each ch around (6 sc). Do not join, work in a spiral.

Rnd 2: Place a marker in 1st st, 2 sc in each sc around (12 sc).

Rnd 3: 2 sc in each sc around (24 sc).

Rnd 4: *Sc in next sc, 2 sc in next sc; repeat from * around (36 sc).

Rnd 5: Sc in each sc around (36 sc).

Rnds 6: *Sc in each of next 2 sc, 2 sc in next sc; repeat from * around, ending with sc in each sc to beginning of rnd (48 sc).

Rnd 7: Sc in each sc around (48 sc).

Rnds 8–9: Rep rnds 6–7 (64 sc).

Rnd 10: *Sc in each of next 3 sc, 2 sc in next sc; repeat from * around, ending with sc in each sc to beginning of rnd (80 sc).

Rnd 11: Sc in each sc around, working 4 increases, evenly spaced around (84 sc).

Rep rnd 11, increasing 4 sc in each rnd until top measures same diameter as sides. Fasten off. Weave in all yarn ends.

FINISHING

Turn sides inside out. With RS facing down, place top over opening on top edge of sides. Tack top in four places around sides. With yarn needle and color A, working through back loops of sts, sew sides to top, easing in fullness. Optional: Sew a favorite button or tassel to center top of hat. You can even sew a row of buttons, evenly spaced, all around the sides of the hat. Or simply pin your favorite brooch to the center front of the hat.

This project was created with

Version 1:

1 skein each of Schoeller Stahl Winter Cotton in black (color A) and turquoise (color B), 60% cotton, 40% acrylic, 1.75oz/50g = 76yd/70m

Version 2:

1 skein each of Schoeller Stahl Winter Cotton in black (color A) and white (color B), 60% cotton, 40% acrylic, 1.75oz/50g = 76yd/70m

Open Diamond
SHELL

DESIGNER:
Deborah Grossman

THE BIG VISUAL APPEAL OF THIS LITTLE SHELL is in the simple, open pattern. And, you can hardly go wrong with bouclé, so there's a feathery flower accent just for kicks.

SKILL LEVEL

Beginner

SIZE

This hat is designed to fit most adult heads.

YOU WILL NEED

- Color A (for hat): 200yd/183m of worsted weight yarn in heathered gray
- Color B (for flower): 10yd/10m of bulky weight bouclé in maroon
- Hooks: 5mm/H-8 and 6.5mm/K-10 1/2 or size needed to obtain gauge

STITCHES USED

Chain stitch (ch)

Double crochet (dc)

Single crochet (sc)

Slip stitch (sl st)

Dc2tog (double crochet decrease): Yo, insert hook into st and draw up a loop, yo and draw through 2 loops, yo, insert hook in next st and draw up a loop, yo, draw through 2 loops, yo, draw through all loops on hook.

Shell: (3 dc, ch 2, 3 dc) in same space.

GAUGE

Take time to check your gauge.

First 2 rnds = 4" in diameter.

14 sts = 4"; 2 rows in shell pattern = 2".

PATTERN NOTES

This hat is worked in the round, from the top down.

Ch 4, sl st in first ch to form ring.

Rnd 1: Ch 3 (counts as dc), 2 dc in ring, ch 1, (3 dc, ch 1) 4 times in ring. Join with sl st in top of ch 3 (5 ch-1 spaces).

Rnd 2: Sl st to next corner ch-1 space, ch 3, (2 dc, ch 2, 3 dc) in same space, ch 2, shell in each ch-1 space around. Join with sl st to top of ch 3 (5 shells).

Rnds 3–7: Sl st to next corner ch-2 space, ch 3, (2 dc, ch 2, 3 dc) in same space, shell in each ch-2 space around. Join with sl st to top of ch 3 (10 shells).

Rnd 8: Sl st to next corner ch-2 space, ch 1, *2 sc in ch-2 space, sc in each of next 6 dc; repeat from * around. Join with sl st in first sc (80 sc).

Rnd 9: Ch 1, *sc in sc, ch 1, sk next sc; repeat from * around. Join with sl st in first sc (40 ch-1 spaces).

Rnds 10–11: Ch 2, (sc, ch 1) in each ch-1 space around. Join with sl st in first sc (40 ch-1 spaces). Fasten off. Weave in all yarn ends.

FIRST FLOWER

With H-8 hook and color B (or color A if a contrast is desired), ch 6, sl st in first ch to form ring.

Rnd 1: Ch 1, work 18 sc in ring. Join with sl st in first sc (18 sc).

Rnd 2: *Ch 3, dc2tog in next 2 sc, ch 3, sl st in next sc; rep from * around, placing last sl st in first sc of Rnd 1. Fasten off. Weave in all yarn ends.

SECOND FLOWER

With K-10 1/2 hook and color B, work same as First Flower.

FINISHING

With RS of each facing up, place smaller flower on top of larger flower, with yarn needle and color A, sew both flowers over the joining sts close to bottom edge of cap as pictured.

This project was created with

1 skein of Spinrite Bernat Berella Muskoka worsted weight yarn in Grey Heather (#9824) (color A), 100% merino wool, 3.5oz/100g = 200yd/182m.

1 skein of Bernat Soft Bouclé bulky weight yarn in Dark Rose (#430) (color B), 98% acrylic/2% polyester, 5oz/140g = 255yd/232m.

Champagne-Taste
Confetti Shell

DESIGNER: Dot Matthews

WHETHER YOU'RE DRESSED UP OR DOWN, you'll find this shell to be perfect, day or night, with most anything in your wardrobe. Use a plain yarn to showcase the attractive, open pattern and scalloped edging.

SKILL LEVEL

Easy

SIZE

This hat is designed to fit most adult heads.

YOU WILL NEED

- 134yd/123m worsted weight yarn
- Hook: 6mm/J-10 or size needed to obtain gauge
- Yarn needle

STITCHES USED

Chain stitch (ch)

Single crochet (sc)

Double crochet (dc)

Treble crochet (tr)

Slip stitch (sl st)

Shell: 5 dc in same st

GAUGE

First 4 rnds = 2½" in diameter

6 sts = 2"

7 rows in pattern = 2"

PATTERN NOTES

This hat is worked in spiraling rounds through rnd 12: Do not join rounds. Use a stitch marker to indicate first stitch in round, move it up at beginning of ea round.

CROWN

Ch 2.

Rnd 1: Work 6 sc in 2nd ch from hook (6 sc). Do not join, work in a spiral.

Rnd 2: Place marker in 1st st, 2 sc in ea sc around (12 sc).

Rnd 3: *Sc in next sc, 2 sc in next sc; repeat from * around (18 sc).

Rnd 4: *2 sc in next sc, sc in ea of next 2 sc; repeat from * around (24 sc).

Rnd 5: *Sc in ea of next 3 sc, 2 sc in next sc; repeat from * around (30 sc).

Rnd 6: *2 sc in next sc, sc in ea of next 2 sc; repeat from * around (36 sc).

Rnd 7: Sc in ea sc around (36 sc).

Rnd 8: *2 sc in next sc, sc in ea of next 5 sc; repeat from * around (42 sc).

Rnd 9: Sc in ea of next 3 sc, *2 sc in next sc, sc in ea of next 6 st; repeat from * 5 times, 2 sc in next sc, sc in ea of last 3 sc (48 sc).

Rnd 10: *Sc in ea of next 7 sc, 2 sc in next sc; repeat from * around (54 sc).

Rnd 11: *2 sc in next sc, sc in ea of next 8 sc; repeat from * around (60 sc).

Rnd 12: *Sc in ea of next 4 sc, 2 sc in next sc; repeat from * around (72 sc). Sl st in next sc to join.

Rnd 13: Ch 4 (counts as tr), working behind ch-4, tr in first sc to the right of ch-4 (crossed tr made), *sk next sc to the left of last crossed tr, tr in next sc, working behind last tr, tr in last skipped sc (crossed tr made); repeat from * around (36 crossed tr). Join with sl st in top of ch 4.

Rnds 14–16: Ch 1, sc in ea st around (72 sc). Join with sl st in 1st sc.

Rnds 17–20: Rep rnds 13-16.

Rnd 21: Ch 3 (counts as dc), 4 dc in same st as join, sk next 2 sc, sc in next sc, sk next 2 sc, *shell in next sc, sk next 2 sc, sc in next sc, sk next 2 sc; repeat from * around (12 shells). Join with sl st in 1st sc. Fasten off. Weave in all yarn ends.

This project was created with

1 ball of Cascade's Tweed Cascade 220 yarn in off white (#7628), 90% Peruvian Highland wool, 10% Donegal, 3.5oz/100g = 220yd/201m.

Julia's COBALT BLUES

DESIGNER:

Jonathan James

DON'T BE FOOLED BY FIRST IMPRESSIONS—this unique hat is multiple hats in one. In its natural state, we admit it's a bit floppy, but with a few well-placed folds, rolls, and twists, this free-form hat can reflect any mood or attire you choose.

SKILL LEVEL

Intermediate

SIZE

This hat is designed to fit most adult heads.

YOU WILL NEED

- Color A: Approx 306yd/28m chunky weight mohair-type yarn in blues
- Color B: Approx 153yd/140m chunky weight multi-colored mohair-type yarn in brown/gold
- Color C: Approx 100yd/91m worsted weight fun-fur type yarn in royal blue
- Color D: Approx 108yd/99m bulky yarn in lilac
- Color E: Approx 100yd/91m bulky chenille yarn in black
- Hooks: 5mm/H-8 and 6.5mm/K-10 1/2 or sizes needed to obtain gauge

STITCHES USED

Chain stitch (ch)

Single crochet (sc)

Elongated Double crochet (edc): Yo, insert hook in next st, yo, draw yarn through st, draw up loops to height of beginning ch 6 (approximately 1¼"), (yo, draw yarn through 2 loops on hook) twice.

Slip stitch (sl st)

GAUGE

Gauge may vary, depending on yarn and hook used. As a guide, use yarns and hooks that will achieve the following gauges:

First 3 rnds = 2" in diameter; 10 sts = 4".

PATTERN NOTES

This hat is a freeform design. Use your choice of any combination of five yarns that work to gauge. Hat is worked in rounds, from the top down.

With H-8 hook and color A, ch 5, sl st in 1st ch to form ring.

Rnd 1: Ch 1, work 10 sc in ring. Join with sl st in 1st sc (10 sc).

Rnd 2: Ch 1, 2 sc in each sc around. Join with sl st in 1st sc (20 sc).

Rnd 3: Ch 1, *sc in each of next 4 sc, 2 sc in next sc; repeat from *

around. Join with sl st in 1st sc (24 sc).

Rnd 4: With K-10 1/2 hook, ch 6 (counts as 1st edc), edc in each sc around. Join with sl st in top of ch 6 (24 edc).

Rnd 5: Ch 1, *sc in each of next 5 sts, 2 sc in next st; repeat from * around. Join with sl st in 1st sc (28 sc).

Rnd 6: Ch 1, *sc in each of next 6 sts, 2 sc in next st; repeat from * around. Join with sl st in 1st sc (32 sc).

Rnd 7: Ch 1, *sc in each of next 7 sts, 2 sc in next st; repeat from * around. Join with sl st in 1st sc (36 sc).

Rnd 8: Ch 6 (counts as 1st edc), edc in each sc around. Join with sl st in top of ch 6 (36 edc). Note: This rnd should measure approximately 15" in circumference.

Rnd 9: Ch 1, *sc in each of next 5 sts, 2 sc in next st; repeat from * around. Join with sl st in 1st sc (42 sc).

Rnd 10: Ch 1, *sc in each of next 6 sts, 2 sc in next st; repeat from * around. Join with sl st in 1st sc (48 sc).

Rnd 11: Ch 6 (counts as 1st edc), edc in each sc around. Join with sl st in

top of ch 6 (48 edc). Note: This rnd should measure approximately 20" in circumference.

Rnd 12: Ch 1, *sc in each of next 7 sts, 2 sc in next st; repeat from * around. Join with sl st in 1st sc (54 sc).

Rnd 13: Ch 1, *sc in each of next 8 sts, 2 sc in next st; repeat from * around. Join with sl st in 1st sc (60 sc).

Rnd 14: Repeat rnd 11 (60 edc). Note: This rnd should measure approximately 24" in circumference.

Rnd 15: Ch 1, sc in each edc around. Join with sl st in 1st sc (60 sc).

Rnd 16: Ch 1, *sc in each of next 5 sts, 2 sc in next st; repeat from * around. Join with sl st in 1st sc (70 sc). Fasten off A, join color B.

Rnd 17: With H-8 hook and color B, ch 1, sc in each sc around. Join with sl st in 1st sc (70 sc).

Rnd 18: Ch 1, *sc in each of next 34 sts, 2 sc in next st; repeat from * around. Join with sl st in 1st sc (72 sc).

Rnd 19: Ch 1, *sc in each of next 35 sts, 2 sc in next st; repeat from * around. Join with sl st in 1st sc (74 sc).

Rnd 20: Ch 1, *sc in each of next 36 sts, 2 sc in next st; repeat from * around. Join with sl st in 1st sc (76 sc). Fasten off B, join color C.

Rnd 21: With H-8 hook and color C, ch 1, sc in each sc around. Join with sl st in 1st sc (76 sc).

Rnd 22: Repeat Rnd 21 (76 sc). Fasten off C, join D.

Rnd 23: With H-8 hook and color D, repeat Rnd 21 (76 sc).

Rnd 24: Ch 1, *sc in each of next 6 sts, 2 sc in next st; repeat from * 9 times, sc in each of last 6 sts. Join with sl st in 1st sc (86 sc).

Rnd 25: Ch 1, *sc in each of next 7 sts, 2 sc in next st; repeat from * 9 times, sc in each of last 6 sts. Join with sl st in 1st sc (96 sc). Fasten off D, join color E.

Rnd 26: With H-8 hook and color E, ch 1, *sc in each of next 8 sts, 2 sc in next st; repeat from * 9 times, sc in each of last 6 sts. Join with sl st in 1st sc (106 sc). Note: This rnd should measure approximately 38" in circumference.

Rnd 27: Ch 1, *sc in each of next 9 sts, 2 sc in next st; repeat from * 9 times, sc in each of last 6 sts. Join with sl st in 1st sc (116 sc). Add color C.

Rnd 28: With H-8 hook and colors C and E held together as one, ch 1, *sc in each of next 10 sts, 2 sc in next st; repeat from * 9 times, sc in each of last 6 sts. Join with sl st in 1st sc (126 sc).

Rnd 29: Ch 1, *sc in each of next 11 sts, 2 sc in next st; repeat from * 9 times, sc in each of last 6 sts. Join with sl st in 1st sc (135 sc). Note: This rnd should measure approximately 46" in circumference.

Rnd 30: Ch 1, sc in each sc around. Join with sl st in 1st sc. Fasten off. Weave in all yarn ends.

This Project was Created with

Approx 306yd/28m chunky weight mohair-type yarn in blues (color A)

Approx 153yd/140m chunky weight multi-colored mohair-type yarn in brown/gold (color B)

Approx 100yd/91m worsted weight fun-fur type yarn in royal blue (color C)

Approx 108yd/99m bulky yarn in lilac (color D)

Approx 100yd/91m bulky chenille yarn in black (color E)

Florence
HOODED SCARF

DESIGNER:

Deborah Grossman

You'll be ready to face whatever Mother Nature has in mind with this hooded scarf. Practical and pretty, the hat is worked flat in two pieces, and then sewn together.

SKILL LEVEL

Intermediate

SIZE

The finished hood will fit most adults.

YOU WILL NEED

- 685yd/626m of DK or baby weight yarn in dark lavender
- Hook: 5mm/H-8 or size needed to obtain gauge
- Yarn needle

STITCHES USED

Chain stitch (ch)

Single crochet (sc)

Double crochet (dc)

GAUGE

(2 dc, ch 2, sc) 4 times in pattern = 4"; 4 rows = 4" in pattern.

PATTERN NOTES

This hat is worked flat in two pieces, which are then sewn together.

SIDE

(Make 2)

Starting at bottom edge of scarf, ch 25 loosely.

Row 1: (Dc, ch 2, sc) in 4th ch from hook (1st shell made), *sk next 2 ch, (2 dc, ch 2, sc) in next ch (shell made); repeat from * across (8 shells).

(Note: Piece should measure approximately 7" long.). Ch 2, turn.

Row 2: (2 dc, ch 2, sc) in each ch-2 space across (8 shells). Ch 2, turn.

Rows 3–40 (or until piece measures approx. 20" from beginning): Repeat row 2. Do not ch 2 at end of Row 40.

HOOD

At end of Row 40, ch 34 loosely.

Row 41: (Dc, ch 2, sc) in 4th ch from hook, * sk next 2 chs, (2 dc, ch 2, sc) in next ch; repeat from * across added ch to scarf body, (2 dc, ch 2, sc) in each ch-2 space across (19 shells). Ch 2, turn.

Rows 42–55: Repeat row 2 (19 shells).

Row 56: (2 dc, ch 2, sc) in each ch-2 space across to last ch-2 space, dc in last ch-2 space (18 shells). Ch 1, turn.

Row 57: (2 dc, ch 2, sc) in each ch-2 space across. Ch 2, turn.

Rows 58–59: Repeat rows 56-57. Fasten off. Weave in all yarn ends. (Note: Last row is top edge of hood.)

FINISHING

Sew 2 sides together, matching sts, working across top edge of hood, down back of hood to beginning of row 41.

This project was created with

5 skeins of Debbie Bliss Baby Cashmerino in lavender (#607), 55% Merino wool/33% Microfibre/12% Cashmere, 1.75oz/50g = 137yd/125m

Town & Country
FELTED BUCKET

DESIGNER: Marty Miller

SKILL LEVEL

Easy

SIZE

The finished hat will fit most adult heads.

FINISHED MEASUREMENTS

Measurements before felting: approx 29" in circumference (approx 12½" from center of crown to edge of brim).

Measurements after felting: approx 22½" in circumference (approx 9½" from center of crown to edge of brim).

YOU WILL NEED

- Color A: Approx 220yd/201m bulky wool yarn
- Color B: Approx 240yd219m mohair blend yarn
- Hook: 10mm/N-15 or size needed to obtain gauge

STITCHES USED

Chain stitch (ch)

Single crochet (sc)

Slip stitch (sl st)

GAUGE

Take time to check your gauge.

With one strand ea of A and B held together as one, 8 sts = 4"; 1st 10 rnds = 9¼", before felting.

LOVE THE LOOK OF A BUCKET HAT? We do too—especially a felted one. This chameleon can change its looks from Bohemian casual, to 9-to-5 professional, to proper high tea, with the addition of a silk scarf or a favorite brooch.

CROWN

With one strand ea of A and B held together as one, ch 2.

Rnd 1: Work 6 sc in the 2nd ch from the hook (6 sc). Do not join, work in spiral

Rnd 2: Place marker in 1st st, 2 sc in ea sc around (12 sc).

Rnd 3: *2 sc in next sc, sc in next sc; repeat from * around (18 sc).

Rnd 4: *2 sc in next sc, sc in ea of next 2 sc; repeat from * around (24 sc).

Rnd 5: *2 sc in next sc, sc in ea of next 3 sc; repeat from * around (30 sc).

Rnd 6: *2 sc in next sc, sc in ea of next 4 sc; repeat from * around (36 sc).

Rnd 7: *2 sc in next sc, sc in ea of next 5 sc; repeat from * around (42 sc).

Rnd 8: *2 sc in next sc, sc in ea of next 6 sc; repeat from * around (48 sc).

Rnd 9: *2 sc in next sc, sc in ea of next 7 sc; repeat from * around (54 sc).

Rnd 10: *2 sc in next sc, sc in ea of next 8 sc; repeat from * around (60 sc). Join with a sl st to 1st sc of round.

Rnd 11: Ch 1, working in back loops only, sc in ea sc around (60 sc). Join (under both loops) with sl st to 1st sc.

Rnds 12–24: Ch 1, working under both loops of sts, sc in ea sc around (60 sc). Join with sl st to 1st sc.

BRIM

Rnd 25: Ch 1, working in back loops only, *2 sc in sc, sc in ea of next 9 sc; repeat from * around (66 sc). Join with sl st to 1st sc.

Rnd 26: Ch 1, working under both loops of sts, *2 sc in next sc, sc in ea of next 21 sc; repeat from * around (69 sc). Join with sl st to 1st sc.

Rnd 27: Ch 1, sc in ea of 1st 11 sc, 2 sc in next sc, *sc in ea of next 22 sc, 2 sc in next sc; repeat from * once, sc in ea of last 11 sc (72 sc). Join with sl st to 1st sc.

Rnd 28: Ch 1, *2 sc in sc, sc in ea of next 23 sc; repeat from * around (75 sc). Join with sl st to 1st sc.

Rnd 29: Ch 1, sc in sc and in ea of next 11 sc, 2 sc in next sc, *sc in ea of next 24 sc, 2 sc in next sc; repeat from * once , sc in ea of next 12 sc (78 sc). Join with sl st to 1st sc. Ch 1.

Rnd 30: Ch 1, *2 sc in next sc, sc in ea of next 25 sc; repeat from * around (81 sc). Join with sl st to 1st sc. Fasten off. Weave in all yarn ends.

FELTING

Place hat in a zippered pillowcase (to protect your machine from wool lint). Set the water level of washing machine on low, and use the hottest water possible. Put in small amount of laundry soap. Add two or more of the following: an old towel or two, old pair of jeans, pair of rubber beach shoes, or a few rubber balls. This gives something for the hat to agitate against. Set washer for the most agitation, and check felting process every 5 minutes. Take bag out before spin cycle. Depending on your washer, and heat of the water, you may have to repeat this process 2 or 3 times. If you do repeat it, drain the water, and refill before starting over. Keep checking felting progress. When hat measures close to the finished measurements desired, pull it into shape and rinse it in a sink with cold water. Try it on— you may have to pull it some more. Put a saucer upside down inside hat to form the crown, and set hat upside down on a sweater rack to dry for a day or two. Remember, felting is not an exact science. Every washing machine will handle it differently. If you have successfully felted another way, by all means use your method.

This project was created with

2 skeins Nashua Handknits Creative Focus Chunky in Salmon (#1636) (color A), 75% Wool, 25% Alpaca, 3.5oz/100g = 110yd/100m.

1 ball Crystal Palace Yarns Kid Merino in Red Cinnamon (#9798) (color B), 28% kid mohair, 28% merino wool, 44% micro Nylon, .9oz/25g = 240yd/219m.

Fuzzy
Kitty Hat

DESIGNER: Emily North

KEEP BOTH YOUR HEAD AND EARS WARM in a playful manner with this comfy hat. A great design for those new to crocheting, it's worked circular from the top edge down, forming an enclosed square shape.

SKILL LEVEL

Beginner

SIZE

This hat is designed to fit a woman's head. If you would like to make it larger, check the size after you've joined the foundation chain, and adjust as needed.

YOU WILL NEED

- Color A: 135yd/123m bulky weight yarn in green
- Color B: 201yd/183m worsted weight in gray (for edging and earflaps)
- Hook: 5mm/H-8 or size needed to obtain gauge
- Stitch markers

STITCHES USED

Chain stitch (ch)

Single crochet (sc)

GAUGE

Take time to check your gauge

10 sts and 12 rows = 4" in sc

PATTERN NOTES

This hat is worked from the top down in spiraling rounds; do not join rounds unless otherwise stated. Use a stitch marker to indicate first stitch in round, move it up at beginning of each

round. The earflaps will be crocheted in rows. The corners of the square create "kitty ears" when worn.

HAT

With color A, ch 24.

Rnd 1 (right side): Sc in 2nd ch from hook, sc in each ch across, working across opposite side foundation ch, sc in each ch across (46 sc). Do not join, work in a spiral.

Rnds 2-23: Place marker in 1st st, sc in each sc around (46 sc). At end of last rnd, join with sl st in next sc. Fasten off A.

EDGING

Rnds 24-26: With RS facing, join color B in any st at center of back of hat. Work in a spiral as before. Place marker in 1st st, sc in each sc around (46 sc). Do not fasten off.

FIRST EARFLAP

Lay hat flat. Place a marker 7 sts to the left of center back. Sc in each st across to marker.

Row 1: Sc in marked sc, sc in each of next 8 sc. Ch 1, turn leaving remaining sts unworked (9 sc).

Rows 2–3: Ch 1, sc in each of next 9 sc. Ch 1, turn (9 sc).

Row 4: Ch 1, sk 1st sc, sc in each sc across. Ch 1, turn (8 sc).

Rows 5–11: Ch 1, sk 1st sc, sc in each sc across. Ch 1, turn (1 sc at end of last row). Fasten off, leaving a 3" length of yarn. Cut a 6" strand of color B.

FRINGE

Weave strand through st at tip of earflap. With ends of fringe even, tie 3 strands in an overhand knot, at base of fringe.

SECOND EARFLAP

Row 1: With RS facing, skip 16 sts to the left of last st made in Row 1 of first earflap, join color B in next st, ch 1, sc in same st, sc in each of next 8 sc. Ch 1, turn leaving remaining sts unworked (9 sc).

Complete same as first earflap. Weave in all yarn ends.

This project was created with

1 ball of Lion Brand's Jiffy in Grass Green (#173), 100% acrylic, 3oz/85g = 135yd/123m.

1 skein of Patrons Canadiana in Dark Grey Mix (#312), 100% Acrylic, 3.5oz/100g =201yd/183m.

Ruffled PILLBOX

DESIGNER: **Paula J. Gron**

SKILL LEVEL

Easy

SIZE

This hat is designed to fit most adult heads.

YOU WILL NEED

- 652yd/596m worsted weight yarn
- Hook: 5.5mm/I-9 or size needed to obtain gauge
- Yarn needle

STITCHES USED

Chain stitch (ch)

Single crochet (sc)

Double crochet (dc)

Slip stitch (sl st)

Sc2tog (single crochet decrease): Insert hook into st and draw up a loop, insert hook in next st and draw up a loop, yo, draw through all loops on hook.

Gauge

First 4 rnds = 2 ½" in diameter

11 sts = 4"

12 rows in sc = 4"

The PILLBOX HAS BEEN UPDATED with an architectural ruffled trim. Turn it up on one side for a jaunty look, or all the way around for cosmopolitan flair. The top is accented with a chunky tassel.

TOP

Starting at center top, ch 2.

Rnd 1 (right side): Work 6 sc in 2nd ch from hook. Join with sl st in top of 1st sc (6 sc).

Rnd 2: Ch 1, 2 sc in each sc around. Join with sl st in top of 1st sc (12 sc).

Rnd 3: Ch 1, *sc in next sc, 2 sc in next sc; repeat from * around. Join with sl st in top of 1st sc (18 sc).

Rnd 4: Ch 1, *sc in each of next 2 sc, 2 sc in next sc; repeat from * around. Join with sl st in top of 1st sc (24 sc).

Rnd 5: Ch 1, *sc in each of next 3 sc, 2 sc in next sc; repeat from * around. Join with sl st in top of 1st sc (30 sc).

Rnd 6: Ch 1, *sc in each of next 4 sc, 2 sc in next sc; repeat from * around. Join with sl st in top of 1st sc (36 sc).

Rnd 7: Ch 1, sc in next sc, 2 sc in next sc, *sc in each of next 2 sc, 2 sc in next sc; repeat from * 10 times, sc in last sc. Join with sl st in top of 1st sc (48 sc).

Rnd 8: Ch 1, sc in next sc, 2 sc in next sc, *sc in each of next 3 sc, 2 sc in next sc; repeat from * 10 times, sc in last sc. Join with sl st in top of 1st sc (60 sc).

Rnd 9: Ch 1, sc in each sc around. Join with sl st in top of 1st sc (60 sc).

Rnd 10: Ch 1, sc in each of next 4 sc, sc2tog in next 2 sts, *sc in each of next 8 sc, sc2tog in next 2 sts; repeat from * 5 times, sc in each of last 4 sc. Join with sl st in top of 1st sc (54 sc). Fasten off. Weave in all yarn ends.

SIDE BAND

Ch 54 and without twisting ch, sl st in 1st ch to form ring.

Rnd 1 (right side): Ch 1, sc in each ch around. Join with sl st in top of 1st sc (54 sc).

Rnds 2–12: Ch 1, sc in each sc around. Join with sl st in top of 1st sc (54 sc). Fasten off. Weave in all yarn ends.

ASSEMBLY

With wrong sides of top and side band tog, working through back loops of sts on last rnd of side band and both loops of sts on last rnd of top, with side band facing, join yarn in any sc, ch 1, sc in each sc around. Join with sl st in top of 1st sc (54 sc). Fasten off. Weave in all yarn ends.

RUFFLED BRIM

Rnd 1: With right side facing, working across opposite side of foundation ch on bottom edge of side band, join yarn in any ch, ch 1, sc in each ch around. Join with sl st in top of 1st sc (54 sc).

Rnd 2: Ch 1, *sc in sc, ch 3, sk next sc; repeat from * around. Join with sl st in top of 1st sc (27 ch-3 spaces).

Rnd 3: Sl st in 1st ch-3 space, (2 dc, sl st) in same ch-3 space, (sl st, 2 dc, sl st) in each ch-3 space around. Join with sl st in top of 1st sc (27 scallops).

Rnd 4: *Ch 6, sl st in next dc, ch 4, sl st in next dc; repeat from * around, sl st at base of 1st ch-6 loop to join (54 loops). Fasten off. Weave in all yarn ends. Create ruffle by pushing ch-4 loops to outside, and ch-6 loops toward side band all around.

TASSEL

Wrap yarn 25 times around 6" piece of cardboard. Remove bundle from cardboard. With a separate strand of yarn, tie bundle tog at one end. Cut opposite end of bundle. Tie a separate strand of yarn several times around top of tassel, ¾" below tied end. Tie tassel to top of hat. Trim ends even.

This project was created with

2 skeins of Coats & Clark's TLC Essentials in Persimmon (#2254), 100% acrylic, 6oz/170g = 326yd/298m.

Glam

LAMÉ BEANIE

DESIGNER: Marty Miller

SKILL LEVEL

Easy

SIZE

This beanie is designed to fit most adult heads.

YOU WILL NEED

- 187 yd/171m of nylon worsted weight yarn
- Hook: 5mm/H-8 hook or size to obtain gauge

STITCHES USED

Chain stitch (ch)

Single crochet (sc)

Double crochet (dc)

Slip stitch (sl st)

GAUGE

Take time to check your gauge.

18 sc = 4"

First 4 rnds = 4" in diameter

PATTERN NOTES

You will be working in the round from the top down. Make the hat as long as you want it, by adding or subtracting rounds. Leave ¾" from the total length for the edging rounds. First ch-4 in rnds 2 through 18 counts as a dc, ch-1. Join each round with a sl st

A GALLERY EXHIBITION FOLLOWED BY DINNER at a trendy French hot spot? No worries—you're up to it wearing this sleek, iridescent cap. Made in a comfy stretch nylon/lamé yarn, if it wasn't for the admiring glances, you might forget you had it on.

in the third ch of the first ch 4. You will be working on the right side of beanie throughout.

CAP

Ch 4, sl st in 1st ch to form ring.

Rnd 1: Ch 3 (counts as dc), 11 dc in ring (12 dc). Join with sl st in top of ch 3.

Rnd 2: Ch 4 (counts as dc, ch 1), sk 1st st, (dc, ch 1) in each dc around. Join with sl st 3rd ch of ch 4 (12 ch-1 spaces).

Rnd 3: Ch 4 (counts as dc, ch 1), dc in same st as joining, ch 1, (dc, ch 1) in next dc, *(dc, ch 1, dc, ch 1) in next dc, (dc, ch 1) in next dc; repeat from * around. Join with sl st 3rd ch of ch 4 (24 ch-1 spaces).

Rnd 4: Ch 4 (counts as dc, ch 1), dc in same st as joining, ch 1, (dc, ch 1) in each of next 2 dc, *(dc, ch 1, dc, ch 1) in next dc, (dc, ch 1) in each of next 2 dc; repeat from * around. Join with sl st 3rd ch of ch 4 (36 ch-1 spaces).

Rnd 5: Ch 4 (counts as dc, ch 1), dc in same st as joining, ch 1, (dc, ch 1) in each of next 3 dc, *(dc, ch 1, dc, ch 1) in next dc, (dc, ch 1) in each of next 3 dc; repeat from * around. Join with sl st 3rd ch of ch 4 (48 ch-1 spaces).

Rnd 6: Ch 4 (counts as dc, ch 1), dc in same st as joining, ch 1, (dc, ch 1) in each of next 4 dc, *(dc, ch 1, dc, ch

1) in next dc, (dc, ch 1) in each of next 4 dc; repeat from * around. Join with sl st 3rd ch of ch 4 (60 ch-1 spaces).

Rnd 7: Ch 4 (counts as dc, ch 1), dc in same st as joining, ch 1, (dc, ch 1) in each of next 5 dc *(dc, ch 1, dc, ch 1) in next dc, (dc, ch 1) in each of next 5 dc; repeat from * around. Join with sl st 3rd ch of ch 4 (72 ch-1 spaces).

Rnd 8: Ch 4 (counts as dc, ch 1), dc in same st as joining, ch 1, (dc, ch 1) in each of next 6 dc, *(dc, ch 1, dc, ch 1) in next dc, (dc, ch 1) in each of next 6 dc; repeat from * around. Join with sl st 3rd ch of ch 4 (84 ch-1 spaces).

Rnds 9: Ch 4 (counts as dc, ch 1), sk 1st st, (dc, ch 1) in each dc around. Join with sl st 3rd ch of ch 4 (84 ch-1 spaces).

Rnds 10–18: Repeat Rnd 9.

Pattern Note: To make cloche longer, continue to repeat rnd 9 until cap measures ¾" less than desired length.

Rnd 19: Ch 1, sc in same st as joining, sc in each ch-1 space and each dc around. Join with sl st to 1st sc (168 sc).

Rnds 20–22: Ch 1, sc in each sc around. Join with sl st to 1st sc (168 sc). Fasten off. Weave in all yarn ends.

FLOWER

Ch 2.

Rnd 1: Work 6 sc in 2nd ch from hook. Join with sl st in front loop of 1st sc (6 sc).

Rnd 2: Working in front loops only, (ch 6, sl st, ch 6, sl st) in 1st sc, (sl st, ch 6, sl st, ch 6, sl st) in each sc around. Join with sl st in back loop of 1st sc.

Rnd 3: Working in back loops only, (ch 8, sl st, ch 8, sl st) in 1st sc, (sl st, ch 8, sl st, ch 8, sl st) in each sc around. Join with sl st in back loop of 1st sc. Do not fasten off.

TENDRILS

Ch 21, sl st in 2nd ch from hook and each ch across, sl st to center back of flower, ch 16, sl st in 2nd ch from hook, sl st in each ch across, sl st to center back of flower, ch 11, sl st in 2nd ch from hook, sl st in each ch across, sl st to center back of flower. Fasten off. Weave in all yarn ends. Pin or sew flower to the sc edging of the hat.

This project was created with

1 ball of Plymouth 24K in variegated purple (#467), 82% Nylon/18% Lamè, 1.75oz/50g =187yd/171m.

Divine SIMPLICITY

DESIGNER:
Dot Matthews

This sleek, head-hugging skullie is the perfect three-season hat. The look is uncomplicated, yet trendy, and is highlighted with a cluster stitch to add definition. To best show off the stitch, select a simple yarn.

SKILL LEVEL

Easy

SIZE

This hat is designed to fit most adult heads.

YOU WILL NEED

- 126yd/115m of worsted weight wool in brown tweed
- Hooks: 6mm/J-10 or size needed to obtain gauge
- Yarn needle

STITCHES USED

Chain stitch (ch)

Double crochet (dc)

Single crochet (sc)

Cluster: (Yo, insert hook in next st and draw up a loop, yo and draw through 2 loops) 4 times in same st, yo, draw through all loops on hook.

Sc2tog (single crochet decrease): Insert hook into st and draw up a loop, insert hook in next st and draw up a loop, yo, draw yarn through all loops on hook.

GAUGE

First 2 rnds = 3"

5 sts = 2"

3 rows in dc = 2"

CROWN

Ch 4.

Rnd 1 (right side): Work 11 dc in 4th ch from hook. Join with sl st in top of ch 4 (12 dc).

Rnd 2: Ch 3 (counts as dc), dc in same st as join, 2 dc in ea dc around. Join with sl st in top of ch 3 (24 dc).

Rnd 3: Ch 3 (counts as dc), dc in same st as join, dc in next dc, *2 dc in next dc, dc in next dc; repeat from * around. Join with sl st in top of ch 3 (36 dc).

Rnd 4: Ch 3 (counts as dc), dc in same st as join, dc in ea of next 2 dc, *2 dc in next dc, dc in ea of next 2 dc; repeat from * around. Join with sl st in top of ch 3 (48 dc).

Rnd 5: Ch 3 (counts as dc), dc in same st as join, dc in ea of next 3 dc, *2 dc in next dc, dc in ea of next 3 dc; repeat from * around. Join with sl st in top of ch 3 (60 dc).

Rnd 6: Ch 3 (counts as dc), dc in ea dc around. Join with sl st in top of ch 3 (60 dc).

Rnd 7: Ch 3 (counts as dc), cluster in next dc, *dc in next dc, cluster in next dc; repeat from * around. Join with sl st in top of ch 3 (30 clusters).

Rnd 8: Ch 1, sc in ea st around. Join with sl st in 1st sc (60 sc).

Rnds 9-12: Rep rnds 7-8 twice.

Rnd 13: Ch 1, sc in 1st 10 sc, sc2tog in next 2 sc, *sc in next 10 sc, sc2tog in next 2 sc; repeat from * around. Join with sl st in 1st sc (55 sts).

Rnds 14-15: Ch 1, sc in each sc around. Join with sl st in 1st sc (55 sts).

Rnd 16: Ch 1, *sc in sc, sk next sc, 4 sc in next sc, sk next sc; repeat from * around. Join with sl st in 1st sc (14 shells). Fasten off. Weave in all yarn ends.

This project was created with

1 ball of Cascade's Cascade 220 yarn in brown (#9408), 100% Peruvian Highland wool, 3.5oz/100g = 220yd/201m.

Retro RASTA

DESIGNER:
Dot Matthews

SKILL LEVEL

Intermediate

SIZE

This hat is designed to fit most adult heads.

FINISHED MEASUREMENTS

Directions are given for size Small. Changes for Large are in parentheses

Hat: 21½ (25)" in circumference

YOU WILL NEED

- Color A: 191yd/175m worsted weight cotton yarn in orange
- Color B: 191yd/175m worsted weight cotton yarn in green
- Color C: 191yd/175m worsted weight cotton yarn in white
- Color D: 191yd/175m worsted weight cotton yarn in brown

- Hook: 6mm/J-10 or size needed to obtain gauge
- Yarn needle

STITCHES USED

Chain stitch (ch)

Single crochet (sc)

Double crochet (dc)

Treble crochet (tr)

Slip stitch (sl st)

BIG AND BEAUTIFUL, this hat looks equally cool on both men and women. Gotta lotta hair? Tuck it in this roomy rasta, have another latte, and take a walk on the wild side.

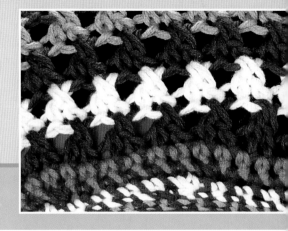

Sc2tog (single crochet decrease) Insert hook in next st and draw up a loop, insert hook in next st and draw up a loop, yo, draw through all loops on hook.

Crossed dc: Skip next st, dc in next st, dc in last skipped st.

GAUGE

Take time to check your gauge

First 4 rnds = 4½" in diameter

9 sts = 4"

PATTERN NOTES

To change color, work last st of 1st color until 2 loops remain on hook, with 2nd color, yo, draw through 2 loops on hook. Fasten off 1st color.

HAT

Rnd 1: Starting at center top of hat, with color A, ch 4 (counts as 1st dc), work 11 dc in 4th ch from hook. Join with sl st in top of ch 4 (12 dc).

Rnd 2: Ch 5, (counts as tr, ch 1), tr in same st as joining, (tr, ch 1, tr) in each dc around. Drop color A, pick up color D. Join with sl st in top of ch 4 (12 ch-1 spaces).

Rnd 3: With color D, ch 1, sc in same st as joining, sc in next ch-1 space, sc in next tr, *sc in next tr, sc in next ch-1 space, sc in next tr; repeat from * around. Drop color D, pick up color C. Join with sl st in 1st sc (36 sc).

Rnd 4: With C, ch 1, *sc in next 2 sc, 2 sc in next sc; repeat from * around. Join with sl st in 1st sc (48 sc).

Rnd 5: Ch 1, *sc in next 3 sc, 2 sc in next sc; repeat from * around. Drop color C, pick up color D. Join with sl st in 1st sc (60 sc).

Rnd 6: With color D, ch 1, *sc in next 4 sc, 2 sc in next sc; repeat from * around. Drop color D, pick up color B. Join with sl st in 1st sc (72 sc).

Rnd 7: With color B, ch 1, *sc in next 5 sc, 2 sc in next sc; repeat from * around. Join with sl st in 1st sc (84 sc).

Rnd 8: Ch 3 (counts as dc), dc in sc to right of joining (last st of previous rnd), *skip next sc, dc in next sc, dc in last skipped sc (crossed dc made); repeat from * around. Drop color B, pick up color D. Join with sl st in top of ch 3 (42 crossed dc).

Rnds 9–17: Rep Rnd 8 working in the following color sequence: 1 rnd each of D, C, D, A, D, B, D, C, D. At end of last rnd, drop D, pick up A.

Rnd 18: With color A, ch 1, sc in same st as joining, sc in each st around. Drop color A, pick up color D. Join with sl st in 1st sc (84 sc).

SIZE LARGE ONLY

Rnd 19: With color D, ch 1, sc in each sc around. Drop color D, pick up color C. Join with sl st in 1st sc (84 sc).

SIZE SMALL ONLY

Rnd 19: With color D, ch 1, *sc in next 5 sc, sc2tog in next 2 sc; repeat from * around. Drop color D, pick up color C. Join with sl st in 1st sc (72 [84] sc).

BOTH SIZES

Rnd 20: With color C, ch 1, *sc in next 4 sc, sc2tog in next 2 sc; repeat from * around. Drop color C, pick up color D. Join with sl st in 1st sc (60 [70] sc).

Rnd 21: With color D, ch 1, *sc in next 5 sc, sc2tog in next 2 sc; repeat from * around. Drop color D, pick up color B. Join with sl st in 1st sc (48 [56] sc).

Rnd 22: With color B, ch 1, sc in each sc around. Drop color B, pick up color D. Join with sl st in 1st sc (48 [56] sc).

Rnd 23: With color D, ch 1, sc in each sc around. Join with sl st in 1st sc (48 [56] sc). Fasten off. Weave in all yarn ends.

This project was created with

1 skein each of Cascade Yarns' Sierra in orange (#54) (color A), green (#08) (color B), white (#01) (color C) and brown (#60) (color D), 80% pima cotton/20% wool, 3.5oz/100g = 191yd/175.

Classic BERET

DESIGNER: Don Halstead

SKILL LEVEL

Intermediate

SIZE

This hat is designed to fit most adult heads.

YOU WILL NEED

- 218yd/200m sport weight wool yarn in blue
- Hook: 5mm/H-8 or size needed to obtain gauge
- Yarn needle

STITCHES USED

Chain (ch)

Single crochet (sc)

Double Crochet (dc)

Treble Crochet (tr)

Sc2tog (single crochet decrease) Insert hook in next st and draw up a loop, insert hook in next st and draw up a loop, yo, draw through all loops on hook.

Dc2tog (double crochet decrease): Yo, insert hook in next st and draw up a loop, yo and draw through 2 loops, yo, insert hook in next st and draw up a loop, yo, draw through 2 loops, yo, draw through all loops on hook.

Tr2tog (treble crochet decrease): *Yo (twice), insert hook in next st and draw up a loop, (yo and draw through 2 loops) twice; repeat from * once, yo, draw through all loops on hook.

THE BERET HAS ENDURED through the ages and has been embraced by both men and women in many cultures. We think the wide attraction is due to its versatility, allowing the wearer a multiplicity of fashionable looks. This design looks fabulous in blue.

GAUGE

Take time to check your gauge.

First 3 rnds = 2¼" in diameter

12 sts = 4"

PATTERN NOTES

This hat is worked from the top down in spiraling rounds; do not join rounds unless otherwise stated. Use a stitch marker to indicate first stitch in round, move it up at beginning of ea round.

Some rounds are worked through both loops, while some rounds are worked through the back loop only. Notations are made for each technique throughout the pattern.

BERET

Starting at center top, ch 3, sl st in first ch to form ring.

Rnd 1: Ch 1, work 6 sc in ring. Do not join, work in a spiral.

Work Rnds 2-9 in back loops only of sts.

Rnd 2: Place marker in 1st st, 1 sc in next sc, 2 sc in each sc around (11 sc).

Rnd 3: Ch 3 (counts as dc), dc in same st as joining, 2 dc in each sc around. Join with sl st in top of ch 3 (22 dc).

Rnd 4: 2 tr in each of next 21 dc, (tr, dc) in next dc (44 sts).

Rnd 5: *Sc in each of next 3 sts, 2 sc in next st; repeat from * around (55 sc).

Rnd 6: *Sc in each of next 4 sts, 2 sc in next st; repeat from * around (66 sc).

Rnd 7: *Tr in next st, 2 tr in next st; repeat from * around to last st, (tr, dc) in last st (99 sts).

Rnd 8: Sc in each st around (99 sc).

Rnd 9: *Dc in next 8 sts, 2 dc in next st; repeat from * around (110 dc).

Work Rnds 10–12 in both loops of sts. Continue to work in a spiral as before.

Rnds 10-12: Sc in each st around (110 sc).

Work Rnds 13-15 in back loops only of sts. Continue to work in a spiral as before.

Rnd 13: *Dc in each of next 8 sts, dc2tog in next 2 sts; repeat from * around (99 dc).

Rnd 14: Sc in each st around (99 sc).

Rnd 15: *Tr in next st, tr2tog in next 2 sts; repeat from * around (66 tr).

Rnd 16: Working in back loops only, *dc in each of next 4 sts, dc2tog in next 2 sts; repeat from * around (55 dc).

BAND

Work Rnds 17–18 in both loops of sts. Continue to work in a spiral as before.

Rnds 17–18: Sc in each st around (55 sc). At end of last rnd, sl st in next sc to join. Fasten off. Weave in all yarn ends.

This project was created with

2 skeins Gjestal Ren NY Ull Superwash Sport Wool in blue, 100% Wool, 1.75oz/50g = 109yd/100m.

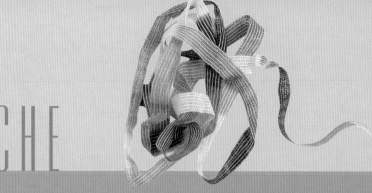

Denim Deco
RIBBON CLOCHE

DESIGNER: Marty Miller

Do your friends know you as a free spirit? Do you believe in good karma? Then this relaxed cloche might fit you to a T. The designer used comfortable ribbon yarn in shades of denim, and popped on an optimistic crocheted sunflower.

SKILL LEVEL

Easy

SIZE

The finished hat will fit most adult heads.

YOU WILL NEED

- 240yd/219m of ribbon yarn in blue variegated for hat (color A)
- 10yd/9m ribbon yarn in white for flower center (color B)
- 50yd/46m of ribbon yarn in yellow for flower petals (color C)
- Hook: 5.5mm/I-9 hook or size needed to obtain gauge

STITCHES USED

Chain stitch (ch)

Single crochet (sc)

Slip stitch (sl st)

GAUGE

Take time to check your gauge.

First 4 rnds = 2" in diameter.

7 sts = 2"

8 rows = 2" in sc.

PATTERN NOTES

You will be working in the round from the top down.

Join ea rnd with a sl st in the 1st sc of that round.

CROWN

With color A, ch 2.

Rnd 1: 6 sc in 2nd ch from the hook (6 sc). Join with sl st to first sc.

Rnd 2: Ch 1, 2 sc in ea sc around (12 sc). Join with sl st to first sc.

Rnd 3: Ch 1, *2 sc in the next sc, sc in the next sc; repeat from * around (18 sc). Join with sl st to first sc.

Rnd 4: Ch 1, *2 sc in next sc, sc in ea of next 2 sc; repeat from * around (24 sc). Join with sl st to first sc.

Rnd 5: Ch 1, *2 sc in next sc, sc in ea of next 3 sc; repeat from * around (30 sc). Join with sl st to first sc.

Rnd 6: Ch 1, *2 sc in next sc, sc in ea of next 4 sc; repeat from * around (36 sc). Join with sl st to first sc.

Rnd 7: Ch 1, *2 sc in next sc, sc in ea of next 5 sc; repeat from * around (42 sc). Join with sl st to first sc.

Rnd 8: Ch 1, *2 sc in next sc, sc in ea of next 6 sc; repeat from * around (48 sc). Join with sl st to first sc.

Rnd 9: Ch 1, *2 sc in next sc, sc in ea of next 7 sc; repeat from * around (54 sc). Join with sl st to first sc.

Rnd 10: Ch 1, *2 sc in next sc, sc in ea of next 8 sc; repeat from * around (60 sc). Join with sl st to first sc.

Rnd 11: Ch 1, *2 sc in next sc, sc in ea of next 9 sc; repeat from * around (66 sc). Join with sl st to first sc.

Rnd 12: Ch 1, *2 sc in next sc, sc in ea of next 10 sc; repeat from * around (72 sc). Join with sl st to first sc.

Rnds 13–30: Ch 1, sc in ea sc around (72 sc). Join with sl st to first sc.

BRIM

Rnd 31: Ch 1, *2 sc in next sc, sc in ea of next 11 sc; repeat from * around (78 sc). Join with sl st to first sc.

Rnd 32: Ch 1, sc in ea of next 6 sc, *2 sc in next sc, sc in ea of next 12 sc; repeat from * around, end with sc in last 6 sc (84 sc). Join with sl st to first sc.

Rnd 33: Ch 1, *2 sc in next sc, sc in ea of next 13 sc; repeat from * around (90 sc). Join with sl st to first sc.

Rnd 34: Ch 1, sc in ea of next 7 sc, *2 sc in next sc, sc in ea of next 14 sc; repeat from * around, ending with sc in last 7 sc (96 sc). Join with sl st to first sc.

Rnd 35: Ch 1, *2 sc in next sc, sc in ea of next 15 sc; repeat from * around (102 sc). Join with sl st to first sc.

Rnd 36: Ch 1, sc in ea of next 8 sc, *2 sc in next sc, sc in ea of next 16 sc; repeat from * around, ending with sc in last 8 sc (108 sc). Join with sl st to first sc.

Rnd 37: Ch 1, *2 sc in next sc, sc in ea of next 17 sc; repeat from * around (114 sc). Join with sl st to first sc.

Rnd 38: Ch 1, sc in ea of next 9 sc, *2 sc in next sc, sc in ea of next 18 sc; repeat from * around, ending with sc in last 9 sc (120 sc). Join with sl st to first sc. Fasten off. weave in all yarn ends.

FLOWER CENTER

With color B, ch 2.

Rnd 1: Work 6 sc in the 2nd ch from the hook (6 sc). Join with sl st to first sc.

Rnd 2: 2 sc in ea sc around (12 sc). Join with sl st to first sc. Fasten off color B.

PETALS

Rnd 3: With RS facing, join color C in front loop of 1st sc in rnd 2, ch 1, working in front loops only of sts, sl st in front loop of 1st sc, *ch 7, sl st in 3rd ch from hook, sl st in ea of next 4 ch sts, sl st in same sc, sl st in next sc; repeat from * around (12 petals). Join with sl st in back loop of 1st sc in rnd 2.

Rnd 4: Working in back loops only of sts in Rnd 2, *ch 9, sl st in 3rd ch from hook, sl st in ea of next 6 ch sts, sl st in same sc of Rnd 2, sl st in next sc of Rnd 2; repeat from * around (12 petals). Join with sl st in first sl st. Fasten off. Weave in all yarn ends.

This project was created with

3 skeins of Crystal Palace's Deco-Ribbon in Jeans (#7237) (color A), 70% Acrylic/30% Nylon, 1.75oz/50 gr = 80yd/73m.

1 skein of Crystal Palace's Deco-Ribbon in white (#300) (color B), 70% Acrylic/30% Nylon, 1.75oz/50 gr = 80yd/73m.

1 skein of Crystal Palace's Deco-Ribbon in yellow (#305) (color C), 70% Acrylic/30% Nylon, 1.75oz/50 gr = 80yd/73m.

Velvet Cabled BEANIE

"MAY I TRY IT ON?" Don't be surprised when your friends ask. And who could blame them? Made of velvety chenille and flaunting a satin silk ribbon, this is one yummy hat.

DESIGNER: Jennifer Hansen

SKILL LEVEL

Advanced

SIZE

This beanie is designed to fit most adult heads.

YOU WILL NEED

- 183yd/167m bulky chenille yarn in copper
- Approx 1 yard of 1½" wide satin silk ribbon to match
- Hook: 6.5mm/K-10 1/2 or size needed to obtain gauge

STITCHES USED

Chain stitch (ch)

Double crochet (dc)

Single Crochet (sc)

Slip stitch (sl st)

Treble Crochet (tr)

Fptr (front post treble crochet): Yo (twice), insert hook from front to back then to front again, around the post of designated st, draw up a loop, (yo and draw through 2 loops on hook) 3 times.

DcTrCL (dc-fptr cluster): Make a cluster in 2 adjacent stitches by working a dc in the first st until 2 loops remain on hook, then yo (twice) and work a tr around the post of the next dc 2 rows below until 3 loops remain on hook (Note: The dc 2 rnds below will either be part of a cluster, or a stand-alone dc), yo, draw through 3 loops on hook. Skip st behind fptr just made.

TrDcCL (fptr-dc cluster): Make a cluster in 2 adjacent stitches by working a fptr around the post of next dc 2 rows below until 2 loops remain on hook, skip st behind tr just made, work a dc in next st in current rnd until 3 loops remain on hook (Note: The dc 2 rnds below will either be part of a cluster, or a stand-alone dc), yo, draw yarn through 3 loops on hook.

GAUGE

Take time to check your gauge.

First 3 rnds = 3½" in diameter

6 sts = 4" in sc

PATTERN NOTES

This beanie is worked from the top down. Where pattern indicates stitches to go around the post of another stitch, work from front to back around the post.

CROWN

Magic Ring: Wrap yarn twice around finger, insert hook in resulting ring, yo, draw yarn through ring, ch 1 to secure.

Rnd 1: Work 8 sc in ring. Use tail of ring to tighten center ring loosely, but leave enough room for hook to pass. Join with sl st in 1st sc (8 sc).

Rnd 2: Ch 3 (counts as dc), *working over rnd 1, tr in center of ring, dc into next sc in rnd 1; rep from * around ending with tr in center of ring. Join with sl st in top of ch 3 (16 sts). Use tail of yarn to fully tighten center ring.

Rnd 3: Ch 1, sc in same st, sc in next tr, sc around the post of same tr, *sc in next dc, sc in next tr, sc around the post of same tr; rep from * around. Join with sl st in 1st st (24 sts).

Rnd 4: Ch 3 (counts as dc), skip 1st sc, fptr around the post of beginning ch 3 (2 rnds below), *dc in next sc, fptr around the post of next tr (2 rnds below same st), skip sc behind fptr just made, dc in next sc, fptr around the post of next tr (2 rnds below), do not skip next sc; rep from * around, omitting last dc and fptr. Join with sl st to top of ch 3 (32 sts).

Rnd 5: Ch 1, *sc in each of next 3 sts, sc in next tr, sc around the post of same tr; repeat from * around. Join with sl st in 1st st (40 sts).

Rnd 6: Ch 3 (counts as dc), skip 1st sc, fptr around the post of beginning ch 3 (2 rows below), *dc in next sc, fptr around the post of next dc (2 rnds below), skip sc behind fptr just made, dc in next sc, fptr around the post of next tr (2 rnds below), do not skip next sc, (dc in next sc, fptr around the post of next tr, skip sc behind fptr just made) twice; rep from * around, omitting last dc and fptr. Join with sl st in top of ch 3 (48 sts).

Rnd 7: Ch 1, *sc in each of next 5 sts, sc in next tr, sc around the post of same tr; rep from * around. Join with sl st in 1st sc (56 sc).

Rnd 8: Ch 3 (counts as dc), skip 1st sc, fptr around the post of beginning ch 3 (2 rows below), *(dc in next sc, fptr around the post of next dc [2 rnds below], skip sc behind fptr just made) twice, dc in next sc, fptr around the post of next tr (2 rnds below same st), do not skip next sc; rep from * around, omitting last dc and fptr. Join with sl st in top of ch 3 (64 sts).

Rnd 9: Ch 1, *sc in each of next 7 sts, sc in next tr, sc around the post of same tr; rep from * around. Join with sl st to 1st sc (72 sts).

Rnd 10: Ch 3 (counts as dc), skip 1st sc, fptr around the post of beginning ch 3 (2 rows below), *(dc in next sc, fptr around the post of next dc [2 rnds below], skip sc behind fptr just made) 3 times, dc in next sc, fptr around the post of next tr (2 rnds below same st), do not skip next sc; rep from * around, omitting last dc and fptr. Join with sl st in top of ch 3 (80 sts).

Rnd 11 (dec rnd): Ch 1, *sc in each of the next 8 sts, sc2tog in next 2 sts; rep from * around. Join with sl st in 1st sc (72 sc).

Rnd 12: Sc around the post of beginning ch 3 (2 rows below) (counts as fptr), skip sc behind st just made, TrDcCl worked across beginning ch 3 (2 rnds below) and next sc (in current rnd), fptr around the post of next dc (2 rnds below), (dc in next sc, fptr around the post of next dc [2 rnds below], skip sc behind fptr just made) twice, DcTrCL worked across next sc and next corresponding dc (2 rnds below), skip next sc, *fptr around the post of next tr (2 rnds below), skip next sc, TrDcCL worked across next corresponding dc (2 rnds below) and next sc (in current rnd), fptr around the post of next dc (2 rnds below), (dc in next sc, fptr around the post of next dc [2 rnds below], skip sc behind fptr just made) twice, DcTrCL worked across next sc and next corresponding dc (2 rnds below), skip next sc; rep from * around. Join with sl st in top of ch 3 (64 sts).

Rnd 13: Ch 1, sc in each of the next 6 sts, sc2tog in next 2 sts; rep from * around. Join with sl st in 1st st (56 sts).

Rnd 14: Sc around the post of beginning ch 3 (2 rows below) (counts as fptr), skip sc behind st just made, skip next sc, *TrDcCL worked across next corresponding dc (2 rnds below) and next sc (in current row), fptr around the post of next dc (2 rnds below), skip sc behind fptr just made, dc in next sc,

fptr around the post of next dc (2 rnds below), skip sc behind fptr just made, DcTrCL worked across next sc and next corresponding dc (2 rnds below), skip next sc, fptr around the post of next tr (2 rnds below), skip next sc; rep from * around, omitting last fptr. Join with sl st in top of ch 3 (48 sts).

Rnd 15: Ch 1, sc in 1st 2 sc, *sc2tog in next 2 sts, sc in each of the next 5 sts; rep from * around, omitting last 2 sc. Join with sl st in 1st st (40 sts).

Rnd 16: Sc around the post of beginning ch 3 (2 rows below) (counts as fptr), skip sc behind st just made, *skip next sc, TrDcCL worked across next corresponding dc (2 rnds below) and next sc (in current row), fptr around the post of next tr (2 rnds below), DcTrCL worked across next sc and next corresponding dc (2 rnds below), fptr around the post of tr (2 rnds below), skip sc behind tr just made; rep from * around, omitting last fptr. Join with sl st in top of ch 3 (32 sts).

Rnd 17: Ch 1, sc in each st around. Join with sl st in 1st sc (32 sts).

Fit beanie to wearer's head and if a smaller size is required, decrease required number of sc in next rnd to achieve the desired fit.

Rnd 18: Ch 1, sc in each sc around, working sc2tog as many times as needed to achieve fit. Join with a sl st to first st.

Rnd 19: Ch 1, sc in each st around. Join with sl st in 1st sc. Fasten off. Weave in all yarn ends.

FINISHING

Weave ribbon through openings in fabric between

sts in rnd 16 as desired. Tie in a loose knot on outside of beanie. Cut excess ribbon.

This project was created with

3 balls of Muench Yarns Touch Me in copper (#3639), 72% rayon/28%wool, 1.75 oz/50g = approx 61 yd/56m

1 yard Hanah Silk 1½" satin silk ribbon in Rusty Bucket (RB)

Luxurious
Hooded Cowl

DESIGNER: Dot Matthews

Lend elegance to any coat or cape with the addition of this graceful wool hood. The incredibly soft mohair trim adds a striking accent. Once you've reached your destination, you can push the hood back to form a cowl.

SKILL LEVEL

Easy

SIZE

This hat is designed to fit most adult heads.

YOU WILL NEED

- Color A: 330yd/302m of worsted weight wool blend in blue-green tweed
- Color B: 21yd/19m of worsted weight mohair blend in cream
- Hooks: 8mm/L-11 (optional for foundation ch), 6.5mm/K-10 1/2 (for wimple) and 5.5mm/I-9 (for trim) or sizes needed to obtain gauge
- Yarn needle

STITCHES USED

Chain stitch (ch)

Double crochet (dc)

Single crochet (sc)

GAUGE

With 6.5mm/K-10 1/2 hook, 6 sts = 2"

7 rows in pattern = 2"

HOOD

With 8mm/L-11 hook and color A, ch 90 and without twisting ch, sl st in 1st ch to form ring.

Rnd 1 (right side): with 6.5mm/K-10 1/2 hook, ch 1, sc in ch, ch 1, sk next ch; repeat from * around (45 ch-1 spaces). Join with sl st in 1st sc, turn.

Rnds 2–50: (Sc, ch 1) in ea ch-1 space around (45 ch-1 spaces). Join with sl st in 1st sc, turn. Fasten off color A.

TRIM

Rnd 51: With RS facing, using 5.5mm/I-9 hook, join color B in any ch-1 space at back of wimple, ch 1, *sc in ch-1 space, sc in next sc; repeat from * around (90 sc).

Rnds 52–54: Ch 1, sc in each sc around. Fasten off B. Weave in all yarn ends.

This project was created with

3 balls of Plymouth Yarns's Suri Merino in blue-green (#791) (color A), 55% Suri Alpaca/45% Extra Fine Merino Wool, 1.75oz/50g = 110yd/100m. 1 ball of Louet Sales' Mohair in cream (#83.1302) (color B), 78% mohair/13% wool/9% nylon, 1.75oz/50gm = 105yd/96m.

Flattop
ZIGZAG HAT

DESIGNER: **Deborah Grossman**

SKILL LEVEL

Intermediate

SIZE

The finished hat will fit most adult heads.

YOU WILL NEED

- Color A: Approx 190yd/173m of worsted-weight wool in fuchsia
- Color B: Approx 190yd/173m of worsted-weight wool in peacock
- Hook: 5mm/H-8 or size needed to obtain gauge
- Yarn needle

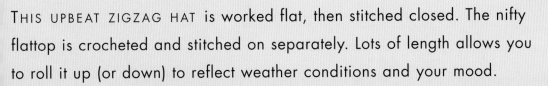
This upbeat zigzag hat is worked flat, then stitched closed. The nifty flattop is crocheted and stitched on separately. Lots of length allows you to roll it up (or down) to reflect weather conditions and your mood.

STITCHES USED

Chain stitch (ch)

Double crochet (dc)

Single crochet (sc)

Slip stitch (sl st)

GAUGE

Take time to check your gauge.

Sides: 14 sts = 4"; 13 rows = 6" in pattern of sides.

Top: First 3 rnds of top = 2½" in diameter; 14 sts and 9 rows = 4" in sc.

PATTERN NOTES

The sides of this hat are worked flat, then stitched closed into a tube. Sides are worked alternating 2 sts of ea color across row. To change color: Work last st of 1st color until 2 lps remain on hook, yo with 2nd color, draw 2nd color through 2 lps on hook; carry 1st color across to be picked up later, working over strand loosely with 2nd color. The top is made separately with 2 colors held together as one, then crocheted to the sides.

SIDES

With color A, ch 37 (or a multiple of 4 + 1 sts to equal desired depth of hat).

Row 1: Sc in 2nd ch from hook, dc in next st, complete last st with B, drop A to be picked up later; with B, sc in next ch, dc in next ch, complete last st with A, drop B to be picked up later; *with A, sc in next ch, dc in next ch, complete last st with B, drop A to be picked up later; with B, sc in next ch, dc in next ch, complete last st with A, drop B to be picked up later; repeat from * across, turn (36 sts).

Row 2: With A, ch 1, *with A, sc in dc, dc in next sc, drop A, pick up B; with B, sc in next dc, dc in next sc, drop B, pick up A; repeat from * across, turn (36 sts).

Repeat row 2 43 more times or until piece measures 21" or desired length to fit around head. With yarn needle, matching sts, sew last row to foundation ch to form a tube.

TOP

With one strand ea of color A and color B held together as one, ch 4, sl st in first ch to form ring.

Rnd 1: Ch 1, work 8 sc in ring (8 sc). Join with sl st in first sc.

Rnd 2: Ch 1, 2 sc in each st around (16 sc).

Rnd 3: Ch 1, *sc in sc, 2 sc in next st; repeat from * around (24 sc).

Rnd 4: Ch 1, *sc in next 2 sc, 2 sc in next st; repeat from * around (32 sts).

Rnd 5: Ch 1, *sc in next 3 sc, 2 sc in next st; repeat from * around (40 sts).

Rnd 6: Ch 1, *sc in next 4 sc, 2 sc in next st; repeat from * around (48 sts).

Rnd 7: Ch 1, *sc in next 5 sc, 2 sc in next st; repeat from * around (56 sts).

Rnd 8: Ch 1, sc in each sc around (56 sts).

Rnd 9 (joining rnd): Place top on one end of side tube, working through double thickness, ch 1, sc evenly around. Join with sl st in first sc. Fasten off. Weave in all yarn ends.

This hat can be worn cuffed once or twice, or uncuffed and slouched over.

This Project was Created with

1 skein of Brown Sheep's Lamb's Pride Worsted weight yarn in Fuchsia (#M23) (color A), 85% wool/15% mohair, 4 oz/113g = 190yd/173m

1 skein of Brown Sheep's Lamb's Pride Worsted weight yarn in Amethyst (#M65) (color B), 85% wool/15% mohair, 4 oz./113g = 190yd/173m

Brilliant
MOROCCAN KUFI

DESIGNER: **Don Halstead**

SKILL LEVEL

Advanced

SIZE

This cap is designed as a men's small.

YOU WILL NEED

- Color A: 108yd/99m of sport weight cotton in tan
- Color B: 108yd/99m of sport weight cotton in orange
- Color C: 108yd/99m of sport weight cotton in brown
- Color D: 108yd/99m of sport weight cotton in red
- Color E: 108yd/99m of sport weight cotton in black
- Color F: 108yd/99m of sport weight cotton in blue
- Hook: 3.75mm/F-5 or size needed to obtain gauge

STITCHES USED

Chain stitch (ch)

Single crochet (sc)

Sc2tog (single crochet decrease): Insert hook into st and draw up a loop, insert hook in next st and draw up a loop, yo, draw through all loops on hook.

CREATE AN EXOTIC KUFI-STYLED CROWNCAP reminiscent of 1920's Morocco. Fashioned in cotton, the exquisite stitch pattern is a great way to use up your stash, and the pattern allows for a shorter version if desired.

GAUGE

Take time to check your gauge 18 sts and 18 rows = 4" in sc

PATTERN NOTES

This cap is made from bottom up, following a chart for color change. The color pattern can easily be adjusted by adding or subtracting multiples of 6 stitches. Always crochet a test swatch first to achieve gauge, and it is advised you try on the cap after about 4 rounds are crocheted to make sure it fits properly. If you need to increase or decrease the size of the cap, increase or decrease the foundation ch in increments of 6 stitches to accommodate the charted pattern.

Sides are worked in 6 colors, following a chart for color changes. Read all rows from right to left, repeating from A to B around. To change color, work last sc of first color until 2 loops remain on hook, yo with second color, draw yarn through 2 loops on hook, drop first color and carry loosely across to be picked up later, work over first color with second color.

CAP

Starting at bottom edge, with color A, ch 90 (or a multiple 6 ch sts to fit snugly around top of head) and without twisting ch, sl st in 1st ch to form ring.

Rnd 1 (right side): Ch 1, sc in each ch around. Join with sl st in 1st sc (90 sc).

Rnd 2: Ch 1, sc in each sc around. Join with sl st in 1st sc (90 sc).

Rnd 3: With color A, ch 1, *with A, sc in next 5 sc, drop A, join B; with B, sc in next sc, drop B, pick up A; rep from * around (Rnd 3 of chart complete). Join with sl st in 1st sc (15 pattern repeats; 90 sc).

Rnds 4–14: Work even in sc following chart for color changes, reading all rows from right to left; repeat from A to B around. Join with sl st in 1st sc (15 pattern repeats; 90 sc). Fasten off

CROWN

Rnd 15: With RS facing, join color A in 1st sc, with A, ch 1, *sc in each of next 4 sc, sc2tog in next 2 sts; repeat from * around, complete last st with color B. Join with sl st in 1st sc (75 sc).

Rnd 16: With color B, ch 1, *with B, sc in sc; with A, sc in each of next 2 sc, sc2tog in next 2 sc; repeat from * around. Join with sl st in 1st sc (60 sc). Fasten off B.

Rnd 17: With color A, ch 1, *sc in each of next 3 sc, sc2tog in next 2 sts; repeat from * around. Join with sl st in 1st sc (48 sc).

Rnd 18: With color A, ch 1, *with A, sc in next 2 sc; with B, sc in next sc; with A, sc2tog in next 2 sc; repeat from * around. Join with sl st in 1st sc (40 sc). Fasten off B.

Rnd 19: With color A, ch 1, *sc in each of next 3 sc, sc2tog in next 2 sts; repeat from * around, complete last st with color B. Join with sl st in 1st sc (32 sc).

Rnd 20: With color B, ch 1, *with B, sc in sc; with A, sc in next sc, sc2tog in next 2 sc; repeat from * around. Join with sl st in 1st sc (24 sc). Fasten off B.

Rnd 21: With color A, ch 1, *sc in each of next 2 sc, sc2tog in next 2 sts; repeat from * around. Join with sl st in 1st sc (18 sc).

Rnd 22: With color A, ch 1, *with A, sc in sc; with B, sc2tog in next 2 sc; repeat from * around. Join with sl st in 1st sc (12 sc). Fasten off B.

Rnd 23: With color A, ch 1, *sc2tog in next 2 sts; repeat from * around. Join with sl st in 1st sc (6 sc). Fasten off, leaving a sewing length. Weave sewing length through last rnd of sts, draw tight and secure. Weave in all yarn ends.

This project was created with

1 skein each of Tahki Cotton Classic in tan (#3204) (color A), orange (#3402) (color B), brown (#3327) (color C), red (#3425) (color D), black (#3002) (color E), and blue (#3871) (color F), 100% mercerized cotton, 1.75oz/50g = 108yd/99m

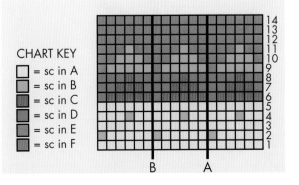

CHART KEY
□ = sc in A
□ = sc in B
▨ = sc in C
▨ = sc in D
■ = sc in E
▨ = sc in F

Peruvian
STOCKING CAP

DESIGNER: **Lindsay Obermeyer**

SKILL LEVEL

Intermediate

SIZE

This hat is designed to fit most adult heads.

YOU WILL NEED

- Color A: 154 yd/137m of worsted weight bouclé wool blend in multi-color
- Color B: 90 yd/82m of worsted weight mohair blend in pink
- Color C: 90 yd/82m of worsted weight mohair blend in salmon
- Hook: 6mm/J-10 or size needed to obtain gauge
- Yarn needle

STITCHES USED

Chain stitch (ch)

Double crochet (dc)

Slip stitch (sl st)

Dc2tog (double crochet decrease) Yo, insert hook into st and draw up a loop, yo and draw through 2 loops, yo, insert hook in next st and draw up a loop, yo, draw through 2 loops, yo, draw through all loops on hook.

GAUGE

12 stitches and 7 rows = 4"

THE COLORFUL TEXTILES OF PERU inspired this warm stocking cap, worked in a bright wool blend with a downy mohair. The snug bouclé earflaps can be worn flipped up, weather permitting.

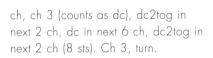

PATTERN NOTES

This hat is worked in rounds using dc in back loops (BL) only. Hat is worked in a stripe pattern in the following color sequence: *2 rows color A, 2 rows color B, 2 rows color A, 2 rows color C; repeat from * through rnd 38.

With color A, ch 60 loosely and without twisting ch, sl st in 1st ch to form ring.

Rnd 1 (right side): Ch 3 (counts as dc), sk 1st ch, dc in each ch around. Join with sl st in top of ch 3 (60 sts).

Rnd 2: Ch 3 (counts as dc), dc in each st around. Join with sl st in top of ch 3 (60 dc). Fasten off color A, join color B.

Rnds 3–11: Maintaining color sequence as established, repeat row 2.

Rnd 12: Ch 3 (counts as dc), dc in next 17 sts, dc2tog in next 2 sts, place a marker in last st, *dc in next 18 sts, dc2tog in next 2 sts, place a marker in last st; repeat from * around. Join with sl st in top of ch 3 (57 sts). Move markers up as work progresses.

Rnd 13: With next color in sequence, ch 3 (counts as dc), dc in each st around. Join with sl st in top of ch 3 (57 dc).

Rnd 14: Ch 3 (counts as dc), dc in each st around, working dc2tog at each marker. Join with sl st in top of

ch 3 (54 sts).

Rnds 15–38: Maintaining color sequence, repeat rnds 13–14 (21 sts at end of last rnd). Fasten off color A at end of last rnd, join color B.

Rnds 39–41: With color B, ch 3, (dc2tog in next 2 sts) around. Join with sl st in top of ch 3 (6 sts at end of last rnd). Fasten off, leaving a sewing length. With yarn needle, weave sewing length through the sts of last rnd, gather sts and secure.

FIRST EARFLAP

Row 1: With right side facing, working across opposite side of foundation ch, join color A in any ch on bottom edge of cap, ch 3 (counts as dc), dc2tog in next 2 ch, dc in next 6 ch, dc2tog in next 2 ch (8 sts). Ch 3, turn.

Rows 2–3: Dc2tog in next 2 sts, dc in ea st across to last 2 sts, dc2tog in last 2 sts (5 sts at end of last row). Ch 3, turn.

Row 4: (Dc2tog in next 2 sts) twice (3 sts). Ch 3, turn.

Row 5: Dc2tog in next 2 sts (2 sts). Fasten off, leaving a sewing length. With yarn needle and sewing length, sew tops of sts together forming a point.

SECOND EARFLAP

Row 1: With right side facing, sk 20 sts to the left of last st made in row 1 of first ear flap, join color A in next

ch, ch 3 (counts as dc), dc2tog in next 2 ch, dc in next 6 ch, dc2tog in next 2 ch (8 sts). Ch 3, turn.

Rows 2–5: Rep rows 2–5 of first earflap. Weave in all yarn ends.

TASSEL

Wrap color A 21 times around 4" piece of cardboard. Remove bundle from cardboard. With a separate strand of color A, tie bundle tog at one end. Cut opposite end of bundle. Tie a separate strand of yarn several times around top of tassel, ½" below tied end. Tie tassel to top of cap.

This project was created with

2 skeins of Noro's Blossom in multi color (#6) (color A), 30% kid mohair/40% wool/20% silk/10% nylon, 1.4oz/40g = 77yd/70m. 1 ball each of Classic Elite's La Gran in Late Summer Rose (#6599) (color B) and Pomegranate (#6565) (color C), 76.5% mohair/17.5% wool/6% nylon. 1.48oz/42gm = 90yd/82m.

Scalloped
TOURING SCARF

DESIGNER:
Lindsay Obermeyer

This ingenious hat is actually a scarf joined in the middle to form a fashionable hood. Imagine yourself zipping along in a sporty convertible with this dramatic headscarf keeping your coif intact. Add a pair of shades, and you're ready for Highway 1.

SKILL LEVEL

Easy

SIZE

This hat is designed to fit most adult heads.

YOU WILL NEED

- Approx 787yd/720m sport weight yarn
- Hook: 4mm/G-6 or size to obtain gauge
- Yarn needle

STITCHES USED

Chain stitch (ch)

Single crochet (sc)

Double crochet (dc)

Slip stitch (sl st)

Scallop: 5 dc in same st.

GAUGE

Take time to check your gauge.

3 scallops = 3¾" in pattern.

10 rows = 4" in pattern.

PATTERN NOTES

This hat is worked flat in 1 piece that resembles a scarf. Scarf is then folded in half and joined across 9" of the back to form the hood.

Ch 56.

Row 1: Sc in 2nd ch from hook, *sk next 2 ch, scallop in next ch, sk next 2 ch, 1 sc in the next ch; repeat from * across (9 scallops). Ch 5, turn.

Row 2: Sk next 2 dc of first scallop, sc in next (center) dc of scallop, *ch 5, skip next 5 sts, sc in next (center) dc of next scallop; repeat from * across ending with ch 2, dc in last sc (8 ch-5 lps). Ch 1, turn.

Row 3: Sc in first dc, *scallop in next sc, sc in next ch-5 lp; repeat from * across, ending with sc in 3rd ch of turning ch (9 scallops). Ch 5, turn.

Repeat rows 2 and 3 until scarf measures 80", ending with row 2 of pattern. Fasten off. Weave in all yarn ends.

FINISHING

Fold scarf in half, matching sts across sides.

BACK SEAM AND SCALLOP EDGING

With RS facing, working through double thickness of scarf halves, matching sts across left side edge, join yarn at folded end, ch 1, sc at fold, *scallop in next row-end dc, sc in next row-end sc; repeat from * to * until 9" from folded end has been joined for back seam. Working through single thickness of front piece of scarf; repeat from * to * across side edge to next corner, working across bottom edge (foundation ch), skip first 3 ch, **scallop in next ch (at base of scallop in row 1), sk next 2 ch, sc in next ch (at base of sc in row 1); repeat from ** across bottom edge to next corner; repeat from * to * across entire front edge to next corner, working across bottom edge (last row of scarf), work scallop in each ch-5 lp across; repeat from * to * across last side edge to back seam, sl st in next sc in base of back seam. Fasten off. Weave in all yarn ends.

This project was created with

8 skeins of Noro's Cash Iroha in garnet (#22), 40% silk/30% lambswool/20% cashmere/10% nylon, 1.4oz/40g = 100yd/91m

Solange Striped
BOARDER CAP

DESIGNER: **Don Halstead**

SKILL LEVEL

Easy

SIZE

This hat is designed to fit most adult heads, somewhat loosely.

YOU WILL NEED

Version 1:

- Color A: 108yd/99m sport weight cotton yarn in medium brown
- Color B: 108yd/99m sport weight cotton yarn in dark charcoal gray

Version 2:

- Color A: 108yd/99m sport weight cotton yarn in dark olive green
- Color B: 108yd/99m sport weight cotton yarn in dark charcoal gray

Both Versions:

- Hook: 3.75mm/F-5 or size needed to obtain gauge
- Yarn needle
- Stitch markers

FROM COLLEGE CAMPUSES TO CITY STREETS, caps like these are all the rage. So wear yours snugly to cover your ears, or roll it up as desired.

STITCHES USED

Chain (ch)

Single crochet (sc)

Slip stitch (sl st)

GAUGE

Take time to check your gauge.

First 4 rnds = 2" in diameter

16 sts = 4"

18 rows = 4" in sc

PATTERN NOTES

This hat is worked from the top down in spiraling rounds; do not join rounds unless otherwise stated. Use a stitch marker to indicate first stitch in round, move it up at beginning of each round.

Cap is worked in a stripe pattern, working in the following color sequence: *2 rnds color A, 2 rnds color B; repeat from * throughout. To change color, work last sc of first color until 2 loops remain on hook, yo with second color, draw yarn through 2 loops on hook, fasten off first color.

Hat is worn with wrong side facing out. Weave in yarn ends on right side.

HAT

Starting at bottom edge, with color A, ch 88 and without twisting ch, sl st in first ch to form ring.

Rnd 1: With color A, ch 1, sc in each ch around (88 sc). Do not join, work in a spiral.

Rnd 2: Place marker in 1st st, sc in each sc around (88 sc). Drop A, pick up B.

Rnds 3–4: With color B, sc in each sc around (88 sc). At end of Rnd 4, drop B, pick up A.

Rnds 5–6: With color A, sc in each sc around (88 sc). At end of Rnd 6, drop A, pick up B.

Rnds 7–14: Rep rnds 3–6 (twice).

Note: For longer cap, repeat rnds 3–4 once more.

CROWN

Continue to work in established color sequence throughout.

Rnd 1: *Sc in each of next 9 sc, sc2tog in next 2 sts; repeat from * around (80 sc).

Rnd 2: Sc in each sc around (80 sc).

Rnd 3: *Sc in each of next 8 sc, sc2tog in next 2 sts; repeat from * around (72 sc).

Rnd 4: Sc in each sc around (72 sc).

Rnd 5: *Sc in each of next 7 sc, sc2tog in next 2 sts; repeat from * around (64 sc).

Rnd 6: Sc in each sc around (64 sc).

Rnd 7: *Sc in each of next 6 sc, sc2tog in next 2 sts; repeat from * around (56 sc).

Rnd 8: Sc in each sc around (56 sc).

Rnd 9: *Sc in each of next 5 sc, sc2tog in next 2 sts; repeat from * around (48 sc).

Rnd 10: Sc in each sc around (48 sc).

Rnd 11: *Sc in each of next 4 sc, sc2tog in next 2 sts; repeat from * around (40 sc).

Rnd 12: Sc in each sc around (40 sc).

Rnd 13: *Sc in each of next 3 sc, sc2tog in next 2 sts; repeat from * around (32 sc).

Rnd 14: Sc in each sc around (32 sc).

Rnds 15–18: *Sc in next sc, sc2tog in next 2 sts; repeat from * around (6 sc at end of last rnd). At end of last rnd, fasten off leaving a sewing length. Weave sewing length through the sts of last rnd. Gather and secure. Weave in all yarn ends. Turn hat inside out to wear.

This project was created with

Version 1:

1 skein each of Tahki Cotton Classic in medium brown (#3248) (color A), and charcoal gray (#3039) (color B), 100% Cotton, 1.75oz/50g = 108yd/99m.

Version 2:

1 skein each of Tahki Cotton Classic in dark olive green (#3734) (color A), and charcoal gray (#3039) (color B), 100% Cotton, 1.75oz/50g = 108yd/99m.

Sky-High BEANIE

DESIGNER: Lindsay Obermeyer

This GENEROUSLY SIZED BEANIE looks great standing tall or slouched over. It's worked in a flat rectangle, sewn together to form a tube, and then cinched at the top.

SKILL LEVEL

Intermediate

SIZE

This hat is designed to fit most adult heads.

YOU WILL NEED

- 405 yd/370m of worsted weight wool
- Hook: 4mm/G-6 or needed size to obtain gauge
- Yarn needle
- Pompon frame

STITCHES USED

Chain (ch)

Single crochet (sc)

Half double crochet (hdc)

Double crochet (dc)

Slip stitch (sl st)

GAUGE

18 sts = 4"

12 rows = 4" in pattern

PATTERN NOTES

This hat is worked in a flat rectangle then sewn together into a tube. Top is then cinched together. Work in back loops (BL) only.

Ch 60.

Row 1: Hdc in 2nd ch from hook, hdc in each ch across (59 hdc). Ch 1, turn.

Row 2: Hdc in ea st across (59 hdc). Ch 1, turn.

Rep row 2 until piece measures 21" from beginning, working a multiple of 4 rows. Fasten off leaving a long sewing length.

FINISHING

Working through back loops of sts in last row, sew last row to foundation ch forming a tube.

Cut a 30" length of yarn. With yarn needle and doubled yarn, weave through the sts around one side of tube and gather together to cinch in top. Sew opening closed. Weave in all yarn ends.

Make a 3" pompom and attach to top of the hat.

BOTTOM EDGING

Rnd 1: Join yarn in any row-end st on bottom edge of hat, ch 1, *sc in row-end st, sk next row-end st, 4 dc in next row-end st, sk next row-end st; repeat from * around. Join with sl st in 1st sc. Fasten off. Weave in all yarn ends.

This project was created with

3 skeins of Manos Del Uruguay variegated yarn in Canyon (#102), 100% wool, 3.5 oz/100g = 135yd/124m

Sawtooth BERET

DESIGNER: Don Halstead

SKILL LEVEL

Intermediate

SIZE

The finished hat will fit most adult heads.

YOU WILL NEED

- Color A: 109yd/100m sport weight wool yarn in rust
- Color B: 109yd/100m sport weight wool yarn in yellow/gold
- Hook: 5mm/H-8 or size needed to obtain gauge
- Yarn needle

STITCHES USED

Chain (ch)

Single crochet (sc)

Sc2tog (single crochet decrease): Insert hook in next st and draw up a loop, insert hook in next st and draw up a loop, yo, draw through all loops on hook.

GAUGE

Take time to check your gauge.

First 4 rnds: = 2½"

6 sts and 6 rnds = 2" in sc

THE DESIGNER SPICED UP THE TRADITIONAL MONOTONE BERET by adding a contrasting second color in a sawtooth design. Its smaller circumference allows it to be worn pushed up in the front.

PATTERN NOTES

This hat is worked from the top down in spiraling rounds; do not join rounds unless otherwise stated. Use a stitch marker to indicate first stitch in round, move it up at beginning of each round.

To change color, work last sc of first color until 2 loops remain on hook, yo with second color, draw yarn through 2 loops on hook, drop first color and carry loosely across to be picked up later, work over first color with second color. Fasten off colors when no longer needed in next round.

BERET

Starting at center top, with color B, ch 3, sl st in first ch to form ring.

Rnd 1: Ch 1, work 7 sc in ring. Do not join, work in a spiral.

Rnd 2: Place marker in 1st st, 2 sc in each sc around (14 sc).

Rnd 3: *2 sc in next sc, sc in next sc; repeat from * around (21 sc).

Rnd 4: *2 sc in next sc, sc in each of next 2 sc; repeat from * around, drop B, join A (28 sc). Fasten off B.

Rnd 5: With color A, *2 sc in next sc, sc in next 3 sc; repeat from * around (35 sc).

Rnd 6: *2 sc in next sc, sc in each of next 4 sc; repeat from * around (42 sc).

Rnd 7: *2 sc in next sc, sc in each of next 5 sc; repeat from * around (49 sc).

Rnd 8: *2 sc in next sc, sc in each of next 6 sc; repeat from * around (56 sc).

Rnd 9: *2 sc in next sc, sc in each of next 7 sc; repeat from * around (63 sc).

Rnd 10: *2 sc in next sc, sc in each of next 8 sc; repeat from * around (70 sc).

Rnd 11: *2 sc in next sc, sc in each of next 9 sc; repeat from * around (77 sc).

Rnd 12: *With A, 2 sc in next sc, drop A, pick up B, with B, sc in each of next 2 sc, with A, sc in each of next 2 sc, with B, sc in each of next 2 sc, with A, sc in each of next 2 sc, with B, sc in each of next 2 sc; repeat from * around (84 sc). Fasten off color A.

Rnd 13: With B, sc in each sc around (84 sc).

Rnd 14: *2 sc in next sc, sc in each of next 11 sc; repeat from * around (91 sc).

Rnd 15: Sc in each sc around (91 sc).

Rnd 16: *2 sc in next sc, sc in each of next 12 sc; repeat from * around (98 sc).

Rnds 17–18: Sc in each sc around (98 sc).

Rnd 19: *Sc2tog in next 2 sts, sc in each of next 12 sc; repeat from * around (91 sts).

Rnd 20: Sc in each sc around (91 sc).

Rnd 21: *Sc2tog in next 2 sts, sc in each of next 11 sc; repeat from * around (84 sts).

Rnd 22: Sc in each sc around (84 sc).

Rnd 23: *With B 1, *sc2tog in next 2 sts, drop B, pick up A, with A, sc in each of next 2 sc, with B, sc in each of next 2 sc, with A, sc in each of next 2 sc, with B, sc in each of next 2 sc, with A, sc in each of next 2 sc; repeat from * around (77 sc). Fasten off B.

Rnd 24: With A, *sc2tog in next 2 sts, sc in each of next 9 sc; repeat from * around (70 sc).

Rnd 25: *Sc2tog in next 2 sts, sc in each of next 8 sc; repeat from * around (63 sc).

Rnd 26: *Sc2tog in next 2 sts, sc in each of next 7 sc; repeat from * around (56 sc).

Rnd 27: Sc in each sc around (56 sc). Fasten off. Weave in all yarn ends.

This project was created with

1 skein each of Gjestal Ren NY Ull Superwash Sport Wool in rust (color A) and gold (color B), 100% Wool, 1.75oz/50g: 109yd/100m.

Flight of Fancy
UKULLIE

DESIGNER: Gwen Blakley Kinsler

SKILL LEVEL

Intermediate

SIZE

This cap is designed to fit most adult heads.

YOU WILL NEED

- Color A: 80yd/74m worsted weight ribbon yarn in light oyster
- Color B: Small amount of worsted weight ribbon yarn in orange
- Color C: Small amount of worsted weight ribbon yarn in olive green
- Color D: Small amount of textural/nubby yarn in coordinating color
- Color E: Small amount of eyelash yarn in copper
- Yarn needle
- Stitch markers
- Small amount of quilt batting
- Sheet of tracing paper
- 4 x 5" piece of ultrasuede fabric
- Matching sewing thread
- Sewing needle
- Hook: 4.5mm/G: 6 or size needed to obtain gauge

STITCHES USED

Chain st (ch)

Single crochet (sc)

Half double crochet (hdc)Double crochet (dc)

Treble crochet (tr)

Très chic accurately describes this fashionable skullcap. It's highlighted by a beautiful, freeform embellishment. Wear it when you want to be noticed.

Slip st (sl st)

Bullion st: Yo 7 times, insert hook in space, draw yarn through space and 7 loops on hook, forming a coil, ch 1. Note: The passage of the hook through the coil is facilitated if the coil is held between the thumb and finger of the left hand as the hook is worked through by the right hand.

GAUGE

Take time to check your gauge.

First 3 rnds of cap = 3" in diameter

16 sc = 4"

Freeform Motif = 3" x 4"

PATTERN NOTES

This scull cap is worked from the top down.

CAP

With color A, ch 4, sl st in first ch to form ring.

Rnd 1 (right side): Ch 1, 4 sc in ring. Join with sl st in first sc (ch 6).

Rnd 2: Ch 1, (sc, ch 5, sc) in 1st sc, ch 5, sc in next sc, ch 5, (sc, ch 5, sc) in next sc, ch 5, sc in next sc, ch 3, dc in 1st sc instead of last ch-5 loop (6 ch-5 loops).

Rnd 3: Ch 1, (sc, ch 5, sc, ch 5) in each loop around, ending with ch 3, dc in 1st sc instead of last ch-5 loop (12 ch-5 loops).

Rnd 4: Ch 1, sc in same loop, ch 5, sc in next loop, ch 5, (sc, ch 5, sc, ch 5) in next loop, *(sc, ch 5) in each of next 2 loops, (sc, ch 5, sc, ch 5) in next loop; rep from * around, ending with ch 3, dc in 1st sc instead of last ch-5 loop (16 ch-5 loops).

Rnd 5: Ch 1, sc in same loop, ch 5, (sc, ch 5, sc, ch 5) in next loop, *(sc, ch 5) in each of next 3 loops, (sc, ch 5, sc, ch 5) in next loop; rep from * twice, sc in next loop, ch 5, sc in next loop, ch 3, dc in 1st sc instead of last ch-5 loop (20 ch-5 loops).

Rnd 6: Ch 1, (sc, ch 5) in each loop around, ending with ch 3, dc in 1st sc instead of last ch-5 loop (20 ch-5 loops)

Rnd 7: Ch 1, *(sc, ch 5, sc, ch 5) in loop, (sc, ch 5) in each of next 4 loops; repeat from * around, ending with ch 3, dc in 1st sc instead of last ch-5 loop (24 ch-5 loops)

Rnds 8–9: Rep Rnd 6 (24 ch-5 loops).

Rnds 10–15: Ch 1, (sc, ch 4) in each loop around, ending with ch 2, dc in 1st sc instead of last ch-4 loop (24 ch-4 loops)

Rnd 16: Ch 1, (sc, ch 4) in each loop around. Join with sl st in first sc (24 ch-4 loops).

Rnd 17: Ch 1, work 4 sc in each ch-4 loop around. Join with sl st to 1st sc (96 sc). Fasten off. Weave in all yarn ends.

FREEFORM MOTIF

PATTERN NOTES

"Freeform Crochet" is just as its name indicates: "freedom" to create as you go. If you crochet a st more or less here and there, it won't matter as long as you like how it looks. If you have not mastered the "tricky" bullion st, substitute it with 6 tr instead of 6 bullion sts in the st indicated. When using Color D, hold 2 strands tog with eyelashes alternating to create a thicker result.

Cut threads of colors not in use while working the motif. To change color, work last st of first color until 2 loops remain on hook, yo with second color, draw yarn through 2 loops on hook, fasten off first color.

With color B, ch 3.

Row 1 (right side): Work 6 bullion sts (optional: work 6 tr) in 3rd ch from hook. Drop B, join A. With A, ch 1, turn.

Row 2: Working in front loops only, with A, sc in each of next 4 sts. Ch 3, turn.

Row 3: Working in back loops only, dc in 1st st, hdc in each of next 2 sts, 2 sc in next st, working across side edge of work, sc in next row-end sc, sc in next row-end dc, drop A, join C, with C, sc in same row-end dc, sc in ch at base of Row 1, sc in next ch. Turn.

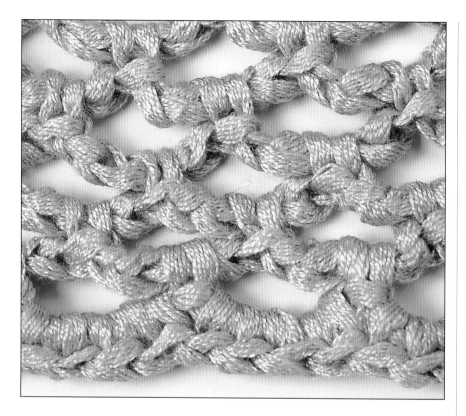

MOTIF BACKING

Lay finished motif on a piece of tracing paper and draw its outline on paper. Cut out paper pattern. Using pattern, cut a piece of fabric to fit on back of motif. Cut a piece of batting, slightly smaller than pattern. Place batting on back of motif and cover it with fabric. With sewing needle and thread, sew fabric to back of motif.

Attach motif to lower right side of cap with bottom edge of motif extending over the edge of cap, being careful to hide sts in motif, and without catching eyelash yarn in sts.

This Project was Created with

1 skein each of Berroco Glace in oyster (#2657) (color A), persimmon (#2520) (color B), and olive pesto (#2567) (color C), 100% rayon viscose, .875 oz/25g = 80yd/74m

1 skein of Berroco Optik in seine (#4918) (color D), 48% cotton/ 21% acrylic/20% mohair/8% metallic/3% polyester, 1.75 oz/50g = 87 yd/80m

1 skein of Berroco Tassel FX in copper black (#3005) (color E), 57% polyester/43% rayon viscose, .875 oz/25g = 80 yd/74m

Row 4: Working in front loops of sts, sl st in each of next 6 sc, sc in next st, 2 sc in next st, hdc in next st, 2 hdc in next, (hdc, dc) in next st. Drop C, join D. Ch 1, turn.

Row 5: Working in back loops only, sc in 1st 4 sts, hdc in each of next 2 sts, (hdc, dc) in next st, 2 dc in next st, dc in next st, hdc in each of next 2 sts, sc in each of next 3 sts, (hdc, dc) in next st, 3 dc in top of beginning ch 3. Ch 1, turn.

Row 6: Working in front loops only, sl st in 1st st, sc in next st (place a marker in this st), sc in each of next 8 sts, hdc in next st, (hdc, dc) in next st, dc in each of next 2 sts, 2 dc in next st, dc in next st, drop D, join 2 strands of color E, with E, holding eyelashes so they fall to front of motif, dc in next st, 2 hdc in next st, sc in each of next 2 sts, 2 sc in next st, working side edge of piece, 2 sc in next row-end sc, sc in each of next 3 row-end sts. Turn.

Row 7: Working in back loops only, sl st in next st, holding eyelashes so they fall to front of motif, sc in each of next 4 sc, 2 sc in each of next 2 sts, sc in next st, drop E, join D, working in both loops, with D, sc in each of next 6 sts, working in back loops only, (sc, hdc) in next st, hdc in each of next 3 sts, sc in next st, drop D, join A, with A, sc in each of next 7 sts, sl st in each of next 3 sts. Turn.

Row 8: Working in front loops only, skip 1st st, sl st in each of next 2 sts, sc in each of next 10 sts, drop A, join B, sc in next st, (sc, hdc) in next st, hdc in next st, 2 hdc in next st, 2 dc in next st, dc in each of next 4 sts, hdc in each of next 5 sts, sc in next st, sl st in next st (place a marker in this st). Fasten off A.

Row 9 (bottom edge): With RS of motif facing, join D in marked sc at beginning of Row 6 (at lower tip of motif), ch 1, working in back loops only, sc in next 9 sts, sl st in next marked st. Fasten off. Weave in all yarn ends.

Festive Olé PILLBOX

THIS VIVID HAT IS A STUNNING SHOWPIECE for any outfit. The snug zigzag brim and variegated crown are worked up separately, and then stitched together.

DESIGNER: Gwen Blakley Kinsler

SKILL LEVEL

Easy

SIZE

This hat is designed to fit most adult heads.

YOU WILL NEED

- Color A: 194yd/177m worsted weight cotton/nylon yarn in variegated colors to coordinate with contrast colors
- Color B: 85yd/78m worsted weight cotton/viscose yarn in red
- Color C: 85yd/78m worsted weight cotton/viscose yarn in turquoise
- Color D: 85yd/78m worsted weight cotton/viscose yarn in hot pink
- Color E: 85yd/78m worsted weight cotton/viscose yarn in yellow
- Color F: 85yd/78m worsted weight cotton/viscose yarn in lime
- Yarn needle
- Sewing needle
- Matching sewing thread
- Hook: 4mm/G-6 or size needed to obtain gauge

STITCHES USED

Chain stitch (ch)

Single crochet (sc).

Half double crochet (hdc)

Slip stitch (sl st)

GAUGE

Take time to check your gauge

Hat: First 5 rnds = 2" in diameter; 9 sts = 2"

Brim: 1 pattern repeat (13 sts) = 2¼"; 7 rows = 2" in sc

PATTERN NOTES

This hat is worked in two pieces that are sewn together. Crown is worked from top down in spiraling rounds; do not join rounds unless otherwise stated. Use a stitch marker to indicate first stitch in round, move it up at beginning of each round. The hat seems large on first few rnds, but begins to draw in on rnds 4 or 5.

The brim is worked in a stripe pattern, working in the following color sequence: *1 rnd each of B, C, D, E, F; repeat from * throughout brim. Starting with rnd 2, brim is worked in back loops only throughout, turning at the end of each rnd.

CROWN

With color A, ch 4 sl st in 1st ch to form ring.

Rnd 1: Work 6 sc in ring (6 sc). Do not join, work in a spiral.

Rnd 2: Place a marker in 1st st, 2 sc in each sc around (12 sc).

Rnd 3: *Sc in next sc, 2 sc in next sc; repeat from * around (18 sc).

Rnd 4: *Sc in each of next 2 sc, 2 sc in next sc; repeat from * around (24 sc).

Rnd 5: Rep rnd 4 (32 sc).

Rnd 6: *Sc in each of next 3 sc, 2 sc in next sc; repeat from * around (40 sc).

Rnd 7: Rep rnd 6 (50 sc).

Rnd 8: *Sc in each of next 4 sc, 2 sc in next sc; repeat from * around (60 sc).

Rnd 9: Sc in each sc around (60 sc).

Rnd 10: Rep rnd 8 (72 sc).

Rnd 11: Sc in each sc around (72 sc).

Rnd 12: Rep rnd 8, ending with sc in each sc to beginning of rnd (86 sc).

Rnd 13: Sc in each sc around (86 sc).

Rnd 14: *Sc in each of next 5 sc, 2 sc in next sc; repeat from * around, ending with sc in each sc to beginning of rnd (100 sc).

Rnds 15–23: Hdc in each st around (100 hdc). At end of last rnd, sc in next st, sl st in next st. Fasten off. Weave in all yarn ends.

BRIM

With color B, ch 120 and without twisting ch, sl st in 1st ch to form ring.

Rnd 1 (right side): Ch 1, 3 sc in 2nd ch from hook (peak made), sc in each of next 5 ch, skip next ch, sc in each of next 5 ch, 3 sc in next ch (peak made); repeat from * around, omitting last 3 sc. Join with sl st in 1st sc, turn (10 pattern repeats). Fasten off B.

Rnd 2 (wrong side): With WS facing, join C in back loop of center sc in 1st peak of last rnd, working in back loops only, ch 1, *3 sc in center sc of peak, sc in each of next 5 sc, skip next 2 sc, sc in each of next 5 sc; repeat from * around. Join with sl st in 1st sc, turn (10 pattern repeats). Fasten off C.

Rnds 3–11: Rep rnd 2, turning at the end of each rnd, working in the following color sequence: 1 rnd each of D, E, F, B, C, D, E, F, B. Fasten off. Mark center back of brim.

FINISHING

It is easiest to fit the two parts of the hat onto your head, stretching brim over crown and placing a "point" of the brim in center of forehead. Pin brim over crown with "dips" between points placed just below crown. Pin generously and remove from head. Sew the two parts together with needle and matching thread from the inside of crown, catching the brim so that stitches don't show on the front.

This project was created with

2 balls of Berroco Zodiac in Taurus (#9635) (color A), 53% cotton/47% nylon, 1.75 oz/50g = 97yd/90m

1 skein each of Berroco Cotton Twist in Flame (#8343) (color B), Gauguin (#8337) (color C), Frankenberry (#8337) (color D), Mirro (#8344) (color E) and Corot (#8339) (color F), 70% mercerized cotton/30% rayon, 1.75 oz/50g = 85yd/78m

Embroidered
RELLIS CAP

DESIGNER:
Paula J. Gron

Practical, yes—fashionable, definitely! The flower-adorned cap hugs your head, while embroidered flaps keep your ears smartly protected from the elements. For added flair, the flap cord ends are punctuated with cabone rings.

SKILL LEVEL

Advanced

SIZE

This hat is designed to fit most adult heads.

YOU WILL NEED

- Color A: 326yd/298m sport weight yarn in beige/gray
- Color B: 136yd/125m fingering weight cotton yarn in purple
- Color C: 136yd/125m fingering weight cotton yarn in blue
- Color D: 136yd/125m fingering weight cotton yarn in turquoise
- Hooks: 4mm/G-6 and 3.5mm/E-4 or sizes needed to obtain gauge
- Yarn needle
- Two ¾" cabone rings
- Color E: 32.8yd/30m #3 pearl cotton in green
- Large-eyed embroidery needle

STITCHES USED

Chain stitch (ch)

Single Crochet (sc)

Half double crochet (hdc)

Double crochet (dc)

Treble crochet (tr)

Double treble crochet (dtr)

Dc2tog (double crochet decrease): Yo, insert hook in next st and draw up a loop, yo and draw through 2 loops, yo, insert hook in next st and draw up a loop, yo, draw through 2 loops, yo, draw through all loops on hook.

EMBROIDERY STITCHES USED

Lazy Daisy Stitch: Bring needle up through fabric at A, form a loop and hold it with your thumb. Insert the needle back down through fabric at A, then bring needle up at B. Make a small anchor stitch on other side of loop to hold the loop in place. Pull gently until loop lays smooth.

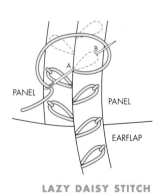

LAZY DAISY STITCH

GAUGE

Take time to check your gauge.

16 sts and 10 rows = 4" in dc

PATTERN NOTES

This cap is constructed in 5 separate panels. Sew together for assembly (wrong sides facing) with seams outward. When folded back at edges for assembly, each panel measures 4". Note right side of work is with tail of beginning chain at left.

PANEL

(Make 5)

With A, ch 29.

Row 1 (right side): Dc in 4th ch from hook, dc in each of next 5 ch, *ch 1, skip next ch, dc in next ch; repeat from * 6 times, dc in each of last 6 ch. Ch 3, turn (27 sts).

Rows 2–12: Skip 1st st, dc in each of next 6 dc, *ch 1, skip next ch-1 space, dc in next dc; repeat from * 6 times, dc in each of last 6 sts. Ch 3, turn (27 sts).

Row 13: Skip 1st st, (dc2tog in next 2 sts) twice, dc in each of next 4 sts, *ch 1, skip next ch-1 space, dc in next dc; repeat from * 4 times, dc in each of next 4 sts, (dc2tog in next 2 sts) twice. Ch 3, turn (23 sts).

Rows 14–15: Skip 1st st, dc in each of next 6 dc, *ch 1, skip next ch-1 space, dc in next dc; repeat from * 4 times, dc in each of last 6 sts. Ch 3, turn (23 sts).

Row 16: Skip 1st st, (dc2tog in next 2 sts) twice, dc in each of next 4 sts, *ch 1, skip next ch-1 space, dc in next dc; repeat from * twice, dc in each of next 4 sts, (dc2tog in next 2 sts) twice. Ch 3, turn (19 sts).

Row 17: Skip 1st st, dc in each of next 6 dc, *ch 1, skip next ch-1 space, dc in next dc; repeat from * twice, dc in each of last 6 sts. Ch 3, turn (19 sts).

Row 18: Skip 1st st, (dc2tog in next 2 sts) twice, dc in each of next 4 sts, ch 1, skip next ch-1 space, dc in each of next 5 sts, (dc2tog in next 2 sts) twice. Ch 3, turn (15 sts).

Row 19: Skip 1st st, dc in each of next 6 dc, ch 1, skip next ch-1 space, dc in each of last 7 sts. Ch 3, turn (15 sts).

Row 20: Skip 1st st, (dc2tog in next 2 sts) twice, dc in each of next 6 sts, (dc2tog in next 2 sts) twice. Ch 3, turn (11 sts).

Row 21: Skip 1st st, (dc2tog in next 2 sts) twice, dc in each of next 2 sts, (dc2tog in next 2 sts) twice. Ch 3, turn (7 sts). Fasten off leaving a 16" sewing length.

EARFLAPS

Row 1: With WS of one panel facing, working across opposite side of foun-

dation ch, join color A in 1st ch, ch 1, sc in each ch across. Ch 3, turn (27 sc).

Row 2: Working in front loops only, skip 1st st, dc in each of next 6 sc, *ch 1, skip next sc, dc in next sc; repeat from * 6 times, dc in each of last 6 sc. Ch 3, turn (27 sts).

Rows 3–7: Working in both loops of sts, skip 1st st, dc in each of next 6 sc, *ch 1, skip next sc, dc in next sc; repeat from * 6 times, dc in each of last 6 sc. Ch 3, turn (27 sts).

Rows 8–9: Repeat Rows 13–14 of panel.

Rows 10–15: Repeat Rows 16–21 of panel. Fasten off.

Repeat earflap on another panel. Weave in all yarn ends.

ASSEMBLY

Fold 7-dc side edges of each panel to RS, at halfway point and pin or baste in place. With WS of panels facing, using yarn needle, and running sts, sew panels together along folded edges, following construction diagram for placement. Sew from bottom of panels to top, drawing tops of last rows together. Note: Folded edges of panels and earflaps will be embroidered later.

HAT EDGING

With RS of hat facing, working across opposite side of foundation ch on back panel, working through double thickness where panels are folded, join color A in 1st available ch on back, ch 1, *sc in each ch across bottom edge of panel(s) to next earflap, fold

earflap down to RS of hat, working in remaining loops of sts in row 1 of earflap, sc in each st across row 1 of earflap; repeat from * around. Join with sl st in 1st sc. Fasten off.

EMBROIDERY

Following diagram for embroidery, with color E and embroidery needle, work embroidery from bottom of earflap up. At outside seams of panels, stitch lazy daisy alternately. Be sure to hide stitching within folded seams as to not show on the reverse (inside). Attach new strands as needed by knotting, and hide ends within stitching.

TIE STRAP

With G-6 hook, join color A at bottom tip of one flap, ch 50 for tie strap, work 22 sc around one cabone ring, sc in each ch back up tie to earflap, sl st in tip of earflap. Fasten off. Weave in all yarn ends.

Repeat tie strap on other earflap.

MAGNOLIA FLOWER

(Make 3, using your choice of any combination of colors B, C and D for 1st, 2nd and 3rd color of each flower).

With E-4 hook and your choice of 1st color, ch 5 and sl st in 1st ch to form ring.

Rnd 1 (right side): Ch 1, work 5 sc in ring. Join with sl st in 1st sc (5 sc).

Rnd 2: Ch 1, 2 sc in each sc around. Join with sl st in 1st sc (10 sc).

Rnd 3: Ch 2 (counts as hdc), hdc in 1st sc, 2 hdc in each sc around. Join with sl st in top of ch 2 (20 sts).

Rnd 4: Working in front loops of sts, *ch 3, tr in same st, 2 tr into each of next 2 hdc, (tr, ch 3, sl st) in next hdc, sl st into next hdc; repeat from *

around (5 petals). Fasten off 1st color.

Rnd 5: With RS facing, working in back loops of sts in rnd 3, join 2nd color in hdc behind the center of any petal, *ch 4, dtr in same st, 2 dtr into each of next 2 hdc, (dtr, ch 4, sl st) in next hdc, sl st into next hdc; repeat from * around (5 petals). Fasten off 2nd color.

Rnd 6: With RS facing, join 3rd color around the post of any sc in rnd 1, ch 1, (sc, ch 3) around the post of each sc around. Join with sl st in 1st sc (5 ch-3 loops). Fasten off. Weave in all yarn ends.

MAGNOLIA LEAF

(Make three)

With E-4 hook and E, ch 16.

Row 1: Sc in 2nd ch from hook, sc in each of next 13 sc, 3 sc in next ch, working across opposite side of foundation ch, sc in each of next 11 ch. Ch 1, turn.

Row 2: Working in back loops of sts, sc in each of next 12 sc, 3 sc in next sc, sc in each of next 10 sc. Ch 1, turn.

Row 3: Working in back loops of sts, sc in each of next 11 sc, 3 sc in next sc, sc in each of next 9 sc. Ch 1, turn.

Row 4: Working in back loops of sts, sc in each of next 10 sc, 3 sc in next

sc (bottom tip), sc in each of next 10 sc. Fasten off. Weave in all yarn ends.

STEMS

With E-4 hook, join color E in center sc at bottom tip of one leaf, ch 10, sl st in center sc at bottom tip of 2nd leaf, ch 30, sl st in center sc at bottom tip of last leaf. Fasten off. Weave in all yarn ends.

FLOWER AND LEAF ASSEMBLY

With color E and large-eyed embroidery needle, fold longer leaf stem in half and sew folded end to tip of back panel (at back of head). Allow leaves to dangle freely down back of cap as pictured. Note the circle of 1st color on the underside of each flower. With right sides up, arrange flowers in a circle on top of cap, with center circles of flowers meeting at center of arrangement. Using matching yarn and running sts, sew flowers to top of cap, working from outer edge of circles to center of arrangement, leaving petals loose. Be sure to join the circular tip of the cap while sewing on flowers.

This project was created with

2 skeins of Patons Katrina in Oyster (#10010) (color A), 92% Rayon/8% Polyester, 3.5oz/100g = 163yd/150m

1 skein each of Patons Grace in Viola (#60322) (color B), Azure (#60104) (color C), Peacock (#60733) (color D), 100% Mercerized Cotton, 1.75oz/50g = 136yd/125m

2 skeins of DMC Pearl Cotton #3 in Blue Green (#502), 100% Mercerized Cotton, 16.4yd/15m

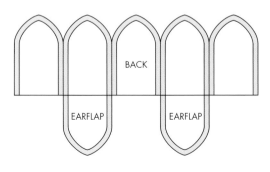

CONSTRUCTION DIAGRAM

Groovin' Granny
SQUARE CLOCHE

DESIGNER: Marty Miller

SKILL LEVEL

Easy

SIZE

This cloche is designed to fit most adult heads.

YOU WILL NEED

- Color A: 77 yd/71m of worsted weight chenille yarn
- Color B: 77 yd/71m of worsted weight chenille yarn
- Color C: 71 yd/65m of mohair blend worsted weight yarn
- Hook: 5.5mm/I-9 or size needed to obtain gauge

STITCHES USED

Chain st (ch)

Single crochet (sc)

Double crochet (dc)

Slip stitch (sl st)

GAUGE

Take time to check your gauge.

Square = 4½" x 4½"

PATTERN NOTES

You will be working only on the right side of the Square. Join each round with a sl st in the third ch of the first ch-3. Start the next round by joining the new color in the ch-1 space at the next corner.

Toss out all of those dusty memories of the Granny Square. Crocheted in incredibly soft (and warm) chenille and mohair yarns, the G. Square has never looked so hip!

CROWN SQUARE

With color A, ch 4, sl st in first ch to form ring.

Rnd 1: Ch 3 (counts as dc), 2 dc in ring, ch 1 (3 dc, ch 1) 3 times in ring. Join with sl st in top of ch 3 (12 dc, 4 ch-1 corner spaces). Fasten off.

Rnd 2: With right side facing, join color B in next corner ch-1 space, ch 3, (2 dc, ch 1, 3 dc, ch 1), in same corner ch-1 space, (3 dc, ch 1, 3 dc, ch 1) in each ch-1 space around. Join with sl st in top of ch 3 (24 dc, 4 corner ch-1 spaces, 4 side ch-1 spaces). Fasten off.

Rnd 3: With right side facing, join color C in next corner ch-1 space, ch 3, (2 dc, ch 1, 3 dc, ch 1) in same corner ch-1 space, ch 1, (3 dc, ch 1) in next ch-1 space, *(3 dc, ch 1, 3 dc, ch 1) in next corner ch-1 space, (3 dc, ch 1) in next ch-1 space; repeat from * around. Join with sl st in top of ch 3 (36 dc, 4 corner ch-1 spaces, 8 ch-1 side spaces). Fasten off.

You will now be connecting the Squares as you make them, on the last round.

SIDE SQUARE 1

Work same as Crown Square through rnd 2.

Rnd 3: With right side facing, join color C in next corner ch-1 space, ch 3, 2 dc in 1st corner ch-1 space, sc in any corner ch-1 space of Crown Square, 3 dc in same corner space of Square 1, sc in next ch-1 space of

Crown Square, 3 dc in next ch-1 space of Square 1, sc in next ch-1 space of Crown Square, 3 dc in corner ch-1 space of Square 1, sc in next corner ch-1 space of Crown Square, 3 dc in same corner ch-1 space of Square 1, ch 1, (you will now be working on Square 1 only) (3 dc, ch 1) in next ch-1 space, *(3 dc, ch 1, 3 dc, ch 1) in next corner ch-1 space, (3 dc, ch 1) in next ch-1 space; repeat from * once. Join with sl st in top of ch 3. Fasten off.

SIDE SQUARE 2

Work same as Crown Square through rnd 2.

Rnd 3: With right side facing, join color C in next corner ch-1 space, ch 3, 2 dc in 1st corner ch-1 space, sc in next corner ch-1 space of Crown Square to the left of Square 1, 3 dc in same corner space of Square 2, sc in next ch-1 space of Crown Square, 3 dc in next ch-1 space of Square 2, sc in next ch-1 space of Crown Square, 3 dc in corner space of Square 2, sc in corner space of Crown Square, sc in corner space of Square 1, 3 dc in same corner space of Square 2, sc in next ch-1 space of Square 1, 3 dc in next ch-1 space of Square 2, sc in next ch-1 space of Square 1, 3 dc in next corner ch-1 space of Square 2, sc in next corner ch-1 space of Square 1, (you will now be working on Square 2 only) (3 dc, ch-1) in same corner space, (3 dc, ch 1) in next ch-1 space, (3 dc, ch 1, 3 dc, ch 1) in next corner space, (3 dc, ch 1) in next sp. Join with sl st in top of ch 3. Fasten off.

SIDE SQUARE 3

Work same as Square 2, connecting Square 3 to Crown Square and Square 2. Fasten off.

SIDE SQUARE 4

Work same as Square 2, connecting Square 4 to Crown Square and Square 3. Also, in the same manner, connect the last side of Square 4 to the first side of Square 1. Fasten off.

BOTTOM BAND

Rnd 1: With right side facing, join color A to any ch-1 space on bottom edge, ch 1, sc in same space, sc in each st and space around. Join with sl st to the first sc. Fasten off.

Rnd 2: With right side facing, join color B in 1st sc, ch 1, sc in each sc around. Join with sl st to the first sc.

Rnds 3-6: Rep rnd 2, working in the following color sequence: 1 rnd each of C, A, B, C. Fasten off. Weave in all yarn ends.

This project was created with

1 skein each of Berroco Chinchilla Taupe (#5103) (color A) and Oyster (#5657) (color B), 100% rayon, 1.75 oz/50g = approx. 77 yd/71m.

1 skein Idena Fame Browns (#200) (color C), 55% acrylic/30% mohair/11% viscose/4% polyester/1.75oz/50g = approx 71 yd/65m.

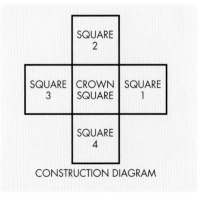

CONSTRUCTION DIAGRAM

Chenille
CHAPKA

DESIGNER: Deborah Grossman

SKILL LEVEL

Intermediate

SIZE

This hat is designed to fit most adult heads.

YOU WILL NEED

- Color A: 200yd/183m super bulky chenille yarn in teal
- Color B: 141yd/129m mixed-fiber worsted weight furry yarn in teal
- Hook: 6mm/J-10 or size needed to obtain gauge
- Yarn needle

STITCHES USED

Chain stitch (ch)

Single crochet (sc)

Slip stitch (sl st)

GAUGE

Take time to check your gauge.

7 sts and 8 rows = 4" in sc

PATTERN NOTES

This hat is worked in sections, starting with the crown. The top is made separately, worked in rnds and sewn to the hat.

THIS FABULOUSLY WARM CHAPKA echoes the Russian military hat worn in the Cold War. This version fights the cold war, too, but with much more style and panache.

CROWN

Starting at top edge of Crown, with colors A and B held together as one, ch 56 and without twisting ch, sl st in first ch to form ring.

Rnd 1: Ch 1, sc in each ch around. Join with sl st in 1st sc (56 sc).

Rnd 2-10: Ch 1, sc in each sc around. Join with sl st in 1st sc (56 sc). Note: Crown should measure 4" from beginning.

TOP

With colors A and B held together as one, ch 4, sl st in first ch to form ring.

Rnd 1: Ch 1, work 8 sc in ring. Join with sl st in first sc (8 sc).

Rnd 2: Ch 1, 2 sc in each sc around. Join with sl st in first sc (16 sc).

Rnd 3: Ch 1, *sc in next sc, 2 sc in next sc; repeat from * around. Join with sl st in first sc (24 sc).

Rnd 4: Ch 1, *sc in each of next 2 sc, 2 sc in next sc; repeat from * around. Join with sl st in first sc (32 sc).

Rnd 5: Ch 1, *sc in each of next 3 sc, 2 sc in next sc; repeat from * around. Join with sl st in first sc (40 sc).

Rnd 6: Ch 1, *sc in each of next 4 sc, 2 sc in next sc; repeat from * around. Join with sl st in first sc (48 sc).

Rnd 7: Ch 1, *sc in each of next 5 sc, 2 sc in next sc; repeat from * around. Join with sl st in first sc (56 sc).

Rnd 8: Ch 1, sc in each sc around.

Join with sl st in first sc (56 sc). Fasten off, leaving a long sewing length.

With sewing length, matching sts, sew top to foundation ch edge of crown.

NECK FLAP

Work now progresses in rows.

Row 11 (RS): Ch 1, sc in each of next 36 sc (36 sc). Ch 1, turn, leaving remaining sts unworked.

Rows 12-18: Sc in each sc across (36 sc). Ch 1, turn. Do not fasten off.

FIRST EARFLAP

Row 19: Ch 1, sc in each of next 8 sc (8 sc). Ch 1, turn, leaving remaining sts unworked.

Rows 20-26: Sc in each sc across (8 sc). Ch 1, turn. Do not ch 1 at end of last row. Fasten off.

SECOND EARFLAP

Row 19: With WS facing, join one strand each of A and B in first sc in Row 18 of Neck Flap, ch 1, sc in each of next 8 sc (8 sc). Ch 1, turn, leaving remaining sts unworked.

Rows 20-26: Sc in each sc across (8 sc). Ch 1, turn. Do not ch 1 at end of last row. Fasten off.

FRONT FLAP

Row 1: With RS facing, skip 1 st to the left of last st made in Row 1 of Neck Flap, join one strand each of A and B in next sc in last rnd of Crown,

ch 1, sc in each of next 18 sc (18 sc). Ch 1, turn, leaving remaining st unworked.

Rows 2-8: Sc in each sc across (18 sc). Ch 1, turn. Do not ch 1, at end of last row. Fasten off. Weave in all yarn ends.

Fold front flap up to right side and tack corners to crown. Attach brooch to center of Front Flap, if desired.

TIE

Cut 4yd length of color A. Fold yarn length in thirds. Loop the tripled piece of chenille through the center two stitches of the one earflap. Cut folded ends creating 6 strands of yarn. Separate into 3 sets of 2 strands of yarn, tightly braid for length of strands. Tie end in an overhand knot and trim even.

Repeat tie on other earflap.

Fold up neck flap and earflaps. Tie ties in a bow on top of hat. In cold weather, untie flaps and tie under chin.

This project was created with

2 skeins of Lion Brand's Chenille Thick and Quick super bulky yarn in Marine (#110) (color A), 91% acrylic/9% rayon, 100yd/91.4m

3 skeins of Patons Allure in Turquoise (#04208) (color B), 100% nylon, 1.75oz/50g = 47yd/43m

Ragg Yarn
WATCH CAP

DESIGNER:
Marty Miller

SEAMEN FIRST POPULARIZED THE WATCH CAP to combat cold, stormy weather during their lookout or "watch" duty. While still performing its job admirably, this design has a healthy helping of rugged good looks.

SKILL LEVEL

Easy

SIZE

This hat is designed to fit most adult heads.

YOU WILL NEED

- Short Hat: 191yd/179m worsted weight ragg yarn in light blue
- Long Hat: 191yd/179m worsted weight ragg yarn in white
- Hook: 5.5mm/I-9 hook or size needed to obtain gauge

STITCHES USED

Chain stitch (ch)

Double crochet (dc)

Slip stitch (sl st)

Front Post Double Crochet (fpdc): Yo, insert hook from front to back to front again, around the post of the next st, yo, draw through st, (yo, draw through 2 loops on hook) twice.

GAUGE

Take time to check your gauge.

First 2 rnds = 3" in diameter.

9 sts = 4"

PATTERN NOTES

You will be working this hat from the crown to the cuff. The body of the hat will be crocheted with RS facing. Once you begin the cuff, you will turn and start working on the WS of the hat, so that when you fold the cuff back, the pattern will be on the outside.

HAT

Rnd 1 (RS): Starting at center top of hat, ch 4 (counts as 1st dc), work 11 dc in 4th ch from hook. Join with a sl st in the top of ch 4 (12 dc).

Rnd 2: Ch 3 (counts as dc), fpdc around the post of same st as joining, (dc, fpdc) in each dc around. Join with a sl st in the top of ch 3 (12 dc, 12 fpdc).

Rnd 3: Ch 3 (counts as dc), dc in same st as joining, fpdc in next fpdc, *2 dc in next dc, fpdc in next fpdc; repeat from * around. Join with a sl st in the top of ch 3 (24 dc, 12 fpdc).

Rnd 4: Ch 3 (counts as dc), dc in same st as joining, fpdc in each of next 2 dc, *2 dc in next dc, fpdc in each of next 2 dc; repeat from * around. Join with a sl st in the top of ch 3 (24 dc, 24 fpdc).

Rnd 5: Ch 3 (counts as dc), dc in same st as joining, dc in next dc, fpdc in each of next 2 fpdc, *2 dc in next dc, dc in next dc, fpdc in each of next 2 fpdc; repeat from * around. Join with a sl st in the top of ch 3 (36 dc, 24 fpdc).

Rnds 6-13: Ch 3 (counts as dc), skip 1st st, dc in each of next 2 dc, fpdc in each of next 2 fpdc, *dc in each of next 3 dc, fpdc in each of next 2 fpdc; repeat from * around. Join with a sl st in the top of ch 3 (36 dc, 24 fpdc).

Note: For longer version, work even for one more rnd.

CUFF

At end of last rnd, turn.

Rnd 14 (WS): Ch 3 (counts as fpdc), skip 1st st, dc in each of the next 2 sts, fpdc in each of next 3 dc, *dc in each of next 2 sts, fpdc in each of next 3 sts; repeat from * around, ending with fpdc in each of the last 2 sts. Join with a sl st in the top of ch 3 (36 fpdc, 24 dc).

Rnds 15-17: Ch 3 (counts as fpdc), skip 1st st, dc in each of the next 2 dc, fpdc in each of next 3 fpdc, *dc in each of next 2 dc, fpdc in each of next 3 fpdc; repeat from * around, ending with fpdc in each of the last 2 fpdc. Join with a sl st in the top of ch 3 (36 fpdc, 24 dc). Fasten off. Weave in all yarn ends.

This project was created with

Short hat: 1 skein Bernat DenimStyle in Stonewash (#117), 70% soft acrylic/30% soft cotton, 3.5oz./100g = 196yd/179m.

Long hat: 1 skein Bernat DenimStyle in Canvas (#006), 70% soft acrylic/30% soft cotton, 3.5oz./100g = 196yd/179m.

Peachy
WAFFLE-WEAVE SHELL

DESIGNER: **Kalpna Kapoor**

NEED A HAT AND NEED IT QUICK? Work up this simple shell hat in a chunky yarn, and you'll be done before you know it.

SKILL LEVEL

Beginner

SIZE

This hat is designed to fit most adult heads.

YOU WILL NEED

- 88yd/80m chunky yarn
- Hook: 5.5mm/I-9 or size needed to obtain gauge
- Yarn needle

STITCHES USED

Chain stitch (ch)

Double crochet (dc)

Slip stitch (sl st)

GAUGE

First 2 rnds = 2¾" in diameter

12 sts = 4"

7 rows in pattern = 4"

CROWN

Starting at center top, ch 4 and sl st in 1st ch to form ring.

Rnd 1: Ch 3 (counts as dc), work 11 dc in ring. Join with sl st in top of ch 3 (12 dc).

Rnd 2: Ch 3 (counts as dc), dc in same st as join, 2 dc in ea dc around. Join with sl st in top of ch 3 (24 dc).

Rnd 3: Ch 3 (counts as dc), 1 dc in same st as join, 2 dc in each of next 2 dc, 1 dc in next dc, *2 dc in each of next 3 dc, 1 dc in next dc; repeat from * around. Join with sl st in top of ch 3 (42 dc).

Rnd 4: Ch 3 (counts as dc), 1 dc in same st as join, ch 1, sk next dc, *2 dc in next dc, ch 1, sk next dc; repeat from * around. Join with sl st in top of ch 3 (21 ch-1 spaces).

Rnd 5: Sl st in 1st ch-1 space, ch 3 (counts as dc), 1 dc in same space, ch 1, (2 dc, ch 1) in each ch-1 space around. Join with sl st in top of ch 3 (21 ch-1 spaces).

Rnds 6–12: Rep rnd 5.

Note: If longer hat is desired, continue to repeat rnd 5 until hat measures desired length. Fasten off. Weave in all yarn ends.

This project was created with

1 ball of Lana Grossa's Multicot Print in tan (#513), 60% cotton, 40% acrylic, 1.75oz/50g = 88yd/80m.

Partial to
PAILLETTES BEANIE

DESIGNER: Deborah Grossman

PAILLETTES ARE ALL THE RAGE. If you like them on purses, you'll love them on hats. Flashy orange ones make this playful hat a show-stopper. It's so easy (and fun) to get a little crazy with this design—just change the yarn color or switch out the sequins.

SKILL LEVEL

Intermediate

SIZE

The finished cloche will fit most adult heads.

YOU WILL NEED

- 60yd/54m heavy worsted weight wool blend yarn in green
- 92 orange 22mm large-hole paillettes
- Hook: 5mm/H-8 or size needed to obtain gauge
- Yarn needle

STITCHES USED

Chain stitch (ch)

Single crochet (sc)

Double crochet (dc)

Slip stitch (sl st)

Single crochet with paillette (spc): Insert hook in back loop of st, yo and draw up a loop (2 loops on hook); draw paillette up close to hook, yo and draw through remaining loops on hook. The paillette will sit on what appears to be the wrong side of the work; cloche will be worn with wrong side facing out.

GAUGE

Take time to check your gauge.

First 4 rnds = 3"

12 sts = 4" in sc

10 rows in sc = 4"

PATTERN NOTES

This cloche is worked from the top down in spiraling rounds; do not join rounds. Use a stitch marker to indicate first stitch in round, move it up at beginning of each round. Work in back loops only throughout. Paillettes must be strung beforehand.

CROWN

Ch 4, sl st in first ch to form ring.

Rnd 1 (wrong side): Ch 1, work 8 sc in ring (8 sc). Do not join, work in a spiral.

Rnd 2: Place marker in 1st st, *2 sc in next st, (sc, spc) in next st; repeat from * around (16 sts, 4 paillettes).

Rnd 3: *Sc in next st, 2 sc in next st; repeat from * around (24 sts).

Rnd 4: *Sc in ea of next 2 sts, 2 sc in next st; repeat from * around (32 sts).

Rnd 5: *Spc in next st, sc in ea of next 2 sts, 2 sc in next st; repeat from * around (40 sts, 8 paillettes).

Rnd 6: *Sc in ea of next 4 sts, 2 sc in next st; repeat from * around (48 sts).

Rnd 7: *Sc in ea of next 5 sts, 2 sc in next st; repeat from * around (56 sts).

Rnd 8: *Spc in next st, sc in ea of next 3 sts, spc in next st, sc in next st, 2 sc in next st) around (64 sts, 16 paillettes).

Rnds 9–10: Sc in each st around (64 sts).

Rnd 11: Sc in ea of next 2 sts, *spc in next st, sc in ea of next 3 sts; repeat from * around to last 2 sts, spc in next st, sc in last sc (64 sts, 16 paillettes).

Rnds 12–13: Sc in each st around (64 sts).

Rnd 14: *Spc in next st, sc in ea of next 3 sts; repeat from * around (64 sts, 16 paillettes).

Rnds 15–16: Sc in each st around (64 sts).

Rnds 17–19: Rep rnds 11–13 (64 sts).

Rnd 20: *Spc in next st, sc in ea of next 3 sts; repeat from * around (64 sts, 16 paillettes). Join with sl st in next sc.

SHELL EDGING

Rnd 21: Ch 1, *sc in sc, sk next st, 5 dc in next st, sk next st; repeat from * around (16 shells). Join with sl st in first sc. Fasten off. Weave in all yarn ends. Turn inside out to wear.

This project was created with

1 ball of Lion Brand Kool Wool in Grass (#130), 50% merino/50% acrylic, 1.75oz/50g = 60yd/54m.

92 orange metallic 22mm large-hole paillettes

elia's Desire

FLAP HAT

DESIGNER: Marty Miller

SKILL LEVEL

Easy

SIZE

This hat will fit most adult heads loosely.

YOU WILL NEED

- Approx 204yd/186m worsted weight yarn
- Hook: 6.5mm/K-10 1/2 or size needed to obtain gauge

STITCHES USED

Chain st (ch)

Single crochet (sc)

Slip stitch (sl st)

Sc2tog (single crochet decrease): Insert hook into st and draw up a loop, insert hook in next st and draw up a loop, yo, draw through all loops on hook.

REPURPOSED FIBER ADDS SUCH INDIVIDUALITY to a garment. Made of recycled sari silk, this earflap hat is a riot of color—sure to put you in a soaring frame of mind. The earflap cords end in fun, nubby knots.

GAUGE

Take time to check your gauge.

First 5 rnds = 4" in diameter.

11 sts and 10 rows sc = 4"

PATTERN NOTES

This hat is worked from the top down in spiraling rounds; do not join rounds unless otherwise stated. Use a stitch marker to indicate first stitch in round, move it up at beginning of ea round. The earflaps will be crocheted in rows. The hanging straps will then be crocheted in rounds.

CROWN

Ch 2.

Rnd 1: 6 sc in 2nd ch from the hook (6 sc). Do not join, work in a spiral.

Rnd 2: Place marker in 1st st, 2 sc in each sc around (12 sc).

Rnd 3: *2 sc in the next sc, sc in the next sc; repeat from * around (18 sc).

Rnd 4: *2 sc in next sc, sc in each of the next 2 sc; repeat from * around (24 sc).

Rnd 5: *2 sc in next sc, sc in each of the next 3 sc; repeat from * around (30 sc).

Rnd 6: *2 sc in next sc, sc in each of the next 4 sc; repeat from * around (36 sc).

Rnd 7: *2 sc in next sc, sc in each of the next 5 sc; repeat from * around (42 sc).

Rnd 8: *2 sc in next sc, sc in each of the next 6 sc; repeat from * around (48 sc).

Rnd 9: *2 sc in next sc, sc in each of the next 7 sc; repeat from * around (54 sc).

Rnd 10: *2 sc in next sc, sc in each of the next 8 sc; repeat from * around (60 sc).

Rnds 11–24: Sc in each sc around (60 sc). At end of rnd 24, sl st to next sc to join, turn.

FIRST EARFLAP

Work now progresses in rows.

Row 1: Ch 1, sc in same sc, sc in ea of next 11 sc, turn (12 sc).

Rows 2–6: Ch 1, sc in ea sc across, turn (12 sc).

Row 7: Ch 1, sc2tog in 1st 2 sts, sc in ea sc across to last 2 sts, sc2tog in last 2 sts, turn (10 sc).

Row 8: Ch 1, sc in ea sc across, turn (10 sc).

Row 9–12: Rep rows 7-8 (twice) (6 sc at end of row 12). Do not turn. Do not fasten off.

FLAP CORD

Pattern note:

Work now progresses in spiral rounds.

You may mark beginning of each round, and move the marker up as work progresses if desired.

Rnd 1: Working from the outside of the cord, bring the first sc of Row 12 around to the last sc of Row 12, sc in the first sc, sc in each sc around (6 sc). Do not join. Work in a spiral.

Rnd 2: Sc in ea sc around (6 sc).

Rep rnd 2 until cord measures approx 10" from beginning and the length of the earflaps and cord is approx 14" from beginning. If you have marked the rounds, finish the last round.

Finishing Cord: *Sc2tog in next 2 sts; repeat from * around and around until 1 sc remains. Fasten off.

SECOND EARFLAP

Rnd 1: With RS facing, sk 14 sts to the left of last st made in row 1 of first earflaps, join yarn to next sc, ch 1, sc in same sc, sc in ea of next 11 sc, turn (12 sc).

FLAP CORD

Work same as first earflap and cord.

Weave in all yarn ends.

This project was created with

1 hank of YarnXPress.com's Sari Silk, 100% recycled Silk, 7oz/200g = 204yd/186m. Note: Color will vary with each hank of Sari Silk.

This cloche was made with hairpin lace, giving it its lovely heirloom, yet oh-so-modern appearance. To produce the long strips of lacy loops, work up the lace on a hairpin lace loom.

SKILL LEVEL

Easy

SIZE

This cloche is designed to fit most adult heads.

YOU WILL NEED

- Color A: 240yd/219m worsted weight rayon yarn in beige multi
- Color B: Approx 210yd/192m worsted weight silk yarn in beige multi
- 2 yards of 1½" satin silk ribbon to match
- Hairpin lace loom that can adjust to the following widths: 1½", 2" and 2½"
- Hooks: 3.75mm/F-5 and 4.5mm/7 or sizes needed to obtain gauge
- Larger hook such as 6.5mm/K-10 1/2 for joining hairpin lace
- ¾" button
- Tapestry needle

STITCHES USED

Chain stitch (ch)

Basic Hairpin Lace Braid

Single Crochet (sc)

GAUGE

Take time to check your gauge.

50 loops = 4"

PATTERN NOTES

- If possible, use an adjustable loom with three configurable prongs that provides a guide for strips with the braid off-center.
- When inserting hook into the hairpin lace loops, insert the hook within the front of the loop from front to back, keeping the loop untwisted.
- When joining hairpin lace strips, always start from the starting edge of the strip to be joined to the existing work. It is always a good practice to create more loops than required in case your count is off. It is always possible to unravel a strip to the desired number of stitches when joining, however, it is very difficult to add additional loops to a strip once it has been removed from the loom.
- Vary location of the joins around the circle to avoid a seam line on the hat.
- For ease, perform joins with large hook, such as K-10 1/2 hook.
- Thread guidelines of contrasting yarn through the hairpin lace strips prior to removing the strips from the loom in order to keep strips untwisted.

CLOCHE

Using smallest hook, leaving 4" tails at beginning and end of each strip, make 9 basic hairpin lace strips as follows:

Strip #1:
With color B, using loom width 2", work 112 loops. Fasten off.

Strip #2: With color A, using loom width 2", work 168 loops. Fasten off.

Strip #3: With color B, using loom width 1 1/2", work 294 loops. Fasten off.

Strip #4: With color A, using loom width 1 1/2", work 294 loops. Fasten off.

Strip #5: With color B, using loom width 1 1/2", work 294 loops. Fasten off.

Strip #6: With color A, using loom width 1 1/2", work 294 loops. Fasten off.

Strip #7: With color A, using loom width 2 1/2", work 294 loops. (Keep the center braid of this strip about 1" in from one of the sides - slightly off center). Fasten off.

Strip #8: With color B, using loom width 2", work 294 loops. Fasten off.

Strip #9: With color A, using loom width 2", work 294 loops. Fasten off.

Taking Strip #1, run an 8" length of scrap yarn through loops on one side of the strip. Tie a firm knot in the scrap yarn, causing the strip to curl upon itself into a circle. The circle should lay flat with starting and ending sides of the strip adjacent to each other. Use the tails of the strip to

weave the start and end of the strip together so that the strip now forms a continuous circle.

For ease, use K-10 1/2 hook or similar large hook for cable joins. This is for ease of joining only, the size of the hook for these joins will not affect the gauge of the work.

JOIN STRIP #1 TO STRIP #2

With a cable join as follows:

With RS facing, insert largest hook through 3 loops on Strip #2, with hook still through these loops on Strip #2, grab the first 2 loops from Strip #1 and pull these 2 loops through the loops on the hook (the 2 loops of Strip #1 remain on the hook); *insert hook through the next 3 loops on Strip #2 and pull these 3 loops through the 2 loops from Strip #1 on the hook (the 3 loops from Strip #2 will remain on the hook); with hook still through these 3 loops from Strip #2, insert hook in next 2 loops on Strip #1 and pull these 2 loops through the 3 loops on the hook (the 2 loops from Strip #1 remain on the hook); repeat from * until the last 2 loops of Strip #1 remain on the hook

and Strip #2 completely encircles Strip #1. Temporarily secure these last 2 loops with a safety pin or locking stitch marker. The starting and ending sides of Strip #2 will lie next to each other. Use the tails of the strip to weave the start and end of the strip together so that the strip now forms a continuous round. Use the tails to mimic the join pattern securing the last 2 loops of the join (from Strip #1) to the first loop of the join.

JOIN STRIP #2 TO STRIP #3

With RS facing, join Strip #3 to Strip #2 in a similar manner as Strip #2 was joined to Strip #1. Join the strips with a cable join as follows: *pick up 3 loops on Strip #3, pick up 2 loops on strip #2, pick up 4 loops on Strip #3, pick up 2 loops on Strip #2; repeat from * across until all loops are joined and 2 loops from Strip #2 remain on hook. Join ends of strips as before.

JOIN STRIP #3 TO STRIP #4

With RS facing, join Strip #4 to Strip #3 in a similar manner as Strip #2 was joined to Strip #1. Join the strips

with a cable join as follows: *pick up 3 loops on Strip #4, pick up 3 loops on Strip #3; repeat from * across until all loops are joined and 3 loops from Strip #3 remain on hook. Join ends of strips as before.

REMAINING JOINS

Join all remaining strips in numerical order, joining 3 loops from each side across same as joining of Strip #3 to Strip #4. When joining the asymmetric strip (Strip #7) be sure to join the side with the longer loops on top, joining to Strip #6, leaving the shorter loops of Strip #7 to be joined to Strip #8. Join ends of each strip as before.

With 4.5/7 hook and WS facing, attach color B with sl st to any loop on the outer edge of Strip #9. Ch 1, keeping loops untwisted, sc in same loop, sc in each loop around. Join with sl st in 1st sc. Weave in all yarn ends.

FINISHING

Weave ribbon between longer loops of strip #7, working over then under each set of 3 loops, one time around

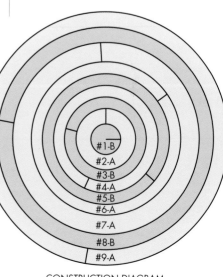

CONSTRUCTION DIAGRAM

cloche; then continue to weave same ribbon under, then over the same loops around. Gather ribbon as needed to achieve proper fit. Secure ends of ribbon on inside of cloche. Cut excess ribbon.

Try on hat, flip up brim to desired height and mark a spot for button. Button will secure the brim of hat through the outer loops of Strip #9. Sew button to front of cloche.

This Project was Created with

1 Hank of Fiesta Yarns Rayon Boucle yarn in Painted Desert (#2120) (color A), 100% Rayon, 4oz/113g = 240yd/219m.

1 Hank of Fiesta Yarns La Luz in Multi Color Painted Desert (#17120) (color B), 100% Silk, 2oz/57g = 210yd/192m.

2yd/1.8m Hanah Silk 1½" satin silk ribbon in Old Ivory (OI)

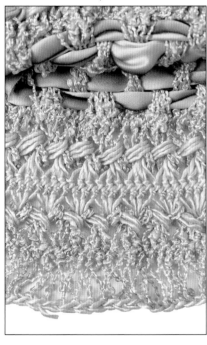

Mr. Wander's

TOP HAT

DESIGNER: Jonathan James

This fantastical hat is definitely wearable art. It was created using freeform crochet—a technique combining various crochet stitches, plus a lot of imagination.

Jonathan must have made quite a dent in his yarn stash creating his top hat! Bulky wool in a rainbow of muted colors is the main ingredient, with subtle touches of novelty yarn serving up unexpected accents. Although intricate in appearance, the hat is made with few stitch types: a blend of double crochet and slip stitch; and the primary stitch, single crochet. The body of the hat was created using increases and decreases to shape it, strategically leaving the front loops free in some rounds for adding the flaps later.

We hope this book has started your creative juices flowing, and that you feel the confidence and inspiration to strike out and create a free-form crochet hat of your own. The free-form aspect ensures that yours will be one of a kind, and that you'll receive many admiring **"where did you get that hat?"** queries.

STITCHES & TECHNIQUES

CONSIDER THIS SECTION YOUR GUIDE TO CROCHET FUNDAMENTALS. Crochet is easy to learn. Throughout this section, the name of a stitch, followed by its abbreviation is given.

CROCHET STITCHES

HOLDING THE HOOK

Before you stitch, you need to get familiar with the hook. There's no right or wrong way to hold it—it's a matter of personal preference. Hold your hook in a manner that you find comfortable. You can hold it like you hold a pencil (figure 1) or like you hold a knife (figure 2). With either method, grip the flattened section of the crochet hook.

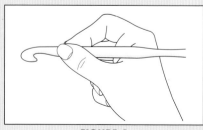

FIGURE 1

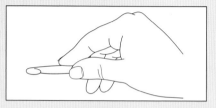

FIGURE 2

MAKING A SLIPKNOT

The first step in crochet is to secure the yarn to the hook. You will do this with a slipknot. Create a loop with your yarn. Leave a tail that measures approximately 6 inches and allow the yarn that's connected to the ball to hang down behind the loop (figure 3). Then, use your hook to pull the yarn from your ball of yarn through the loop. Tighten the slipknot by gently tugging on both yarn ends (figure 4). The loop should move easily on the hook without falling off.

FIGURE 3

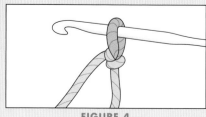

FIGURE 4

HOLDING THE YARN

Holding the yarn to maintain an even yarn tension is the most difficult and frustrating part of learning to crochet. Relax. Like all things, you improve with practice, practice, and even more practice. Experts at crochet will tell you that yarn tension varies from person to person, from day to day, and is even influenced by the mood you're in at the moment.

Wrap the yarn counterclockwise around your little finger. Bring the yarn under your ring and middle finger and over your index finger (figure 5).

As you start to crochet, grasp the slipknot with your thumb and middle finger. As you lift or lower your index finger, you control the tension of the yarn (figure 6). The yarn should be taut enough that you can easily grab it with the end of the hook, but not so taut that you struggle pulling the yarn and hook through your stitch. An easy way to practice controlling yarn ten-

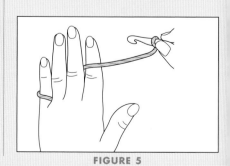

FIGURE 5

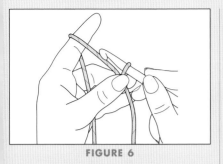

FIGURE 6

sion without starting a project is to make a simple chain.

MAKING A CHAIN

The foundation of every crochet project is a length of chain stitches (chs). You'll crochet the rows or rounds (rnds) of your project on top of this foundation chain.

Make a slipknot on your hook. Holding your hook, bring the yarn over the hook from back to front. Bring the yarn through the loop (lp) on your hook. At the same time, you'll notice that the loop on your hook has slipped off. You've made one chain!

Be sure to work your chain stitches on the thickest part of the crochet hook between where you grasp the hook and the end of the hook. This will ensure that your stitches are not too tight.

Now repeat that series of steps over and over again. As you make new chain stitches, move your thumb and middle finger—of the hand not hold-

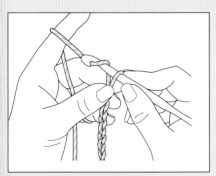

FIGURE 7

ing the hook—up to hold the work (figure 7).

Making a chain is the perfect way to practice maintaining even tension and creating even stitches. You can make a chain and quickly unravel the stitches to start again. With practice, your hands will begin to feel comfortable making the chain. Soon you'll be able to crochet a chain of any length with well-defined chain stitches.

COUNTING CHAIN STITCHES

The first step of any crochet pattern consists of a foundation chain made of a set number of stitches. As you crochet a foundation chain, it's essential to count the number of stitches in the chain. Jot down the number of stitches when you've finished making a chain, then count them again just to be sure.

You'll notice that your chain has two distinct sides. The front of the chain—the right side (RS)—should appear as a series of well-defined V-shapes. The wrong side (WS) appears as a series of small bumpy loops. Hold the chain with the right side of the chain stitches facing you. Start counting with the last stitch you completed (not the one on your hook) and don't count the slipknot you made at the beginning of the chain (figure 8).

If your stitch count matches the number of chain stitches specified in the pattern, you're ready to crochet.

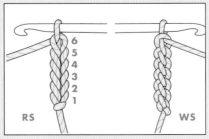

FIGURE 8

SINGLE CROCHET

Single crochet (sc) is a short, basic stitch. To work a row of single crochet stitches, begin with a foundation chain of any number of stitches.

1. Find the second chain stitch from the crochet hook. Insert the point of the hook under the two top loops of the chain stitch (figure 9).

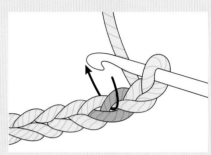

FIGURE 9

2. Bring the yarn over (yo) the crochet hook, catch the yarn, and pull it through the loop on the hook (figure 10). You will now have two loops on your hook.

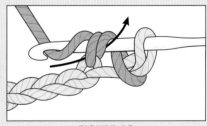

FIGURE 10

3. Bring the yarn over the hook again, grab the yarn with the hook, and pull the yarn through both loops (figure 11). You've completed your first single crochet stitch.

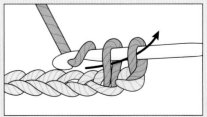

FIGURE 11

4. Insert your hook in the next chain stitch and repeat the steps to create another single crochet (figure 12).

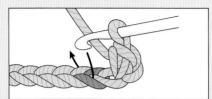

FIGURE 12

TURNING YOUR WORK

Once you've worked to the end of the first row, you'll need to turn your work around to start the next row of stitches. Rotate your work clockwise if you're holding the hook with your right hand, counterclockwise if you're holding it with your left hand (figure 13).

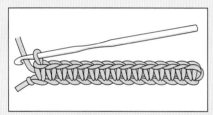

FIGURE 13

Keep the last loop on your hook and turn the completed row so it's under the hand that is holding the yarn. When you do this you'll be able to hold the work between the thumb and middle finger as you work the row.

After you turn the work, you'll need to make a turning chain. A turning chain brings your yarn to the height necessary for the type of stitch you're making in the next row. It will count as the first stitch in the next row. The number of chain stitches you'll need to make for your turning chain depends on what type of stitch you're working in the next row (figure 14).

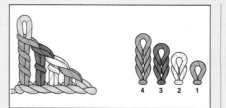

FIGURE 14

After you make your turning chain, insert the hook from front to back underneath the top two loops of the stitch specified in the pattern. Crochet across the row as directed in your pattern.

RIGHT SIDE VS. WRONG SIDE

As you create your crocheted fabric, it will have a right side (RS) and a wrong side (WS). They look somewhat alike, so how do you tell the difference between the two? Your first complete row of stitches (don't count your foundation chain) is the right side. Another way you can distinguish between the right and wrong sides is to look for the tail of the foundation chain. If you're right handed, the tail of the foundation chain will hang on the left and mark the right side. If you're left handed, the tail of the chain will hang on the right and mark the right side.

COUNTING STITCHES

Don't assume that counting stitches is something only an amateur would do. Even experts at crochet count their stitches. It's the only way to insure that you're following a pattern exactly.

You already know how to count chain stitches in a foundation chain (see page 115). To count your crochet stitches in a completed row, lay your work on a flat surface. When there is no decreasing, you can count the ver-

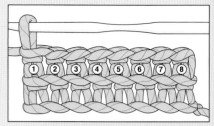

FIGURE 15

tical part—the post (P)—of each crochet stitch (see figure 15). If decreasing is done, the number of posts won't match the number of stitches, so it's better to count the tops of the stitches.

It's a good idea to check your stitch count periodically. This is especially true if you're increasing or decreasing the number of stitches in a row (see pages 122 and 123).

DOUBLE CROCHET

The double crochet stitch (dc) is the workhorse of crochet. It's about twice as tall as the single crochet stitch. Combining the double crochet stitch with other stitches produces different patterns and textures.

1. Make a foundation chain of any number of stitches. Bring the yarn over the hook and insert the hook into the fourth chain from the hook (figure 16).

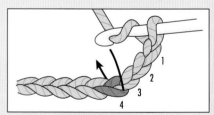

FIGURE 16

2. Bring the yarn over the hook and pull the yarn through the chain stitch. You'll have three loops on your hook (figure 17).

3. Bring the yarn over the hook and draw the yarn through the first two loops on the hook (figure 18). You'll have two loops on your hook.

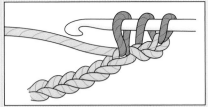

FIGURE 17

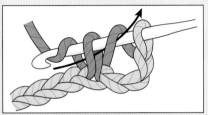

FIGURE 18

4. Bring the yarn over the hook once more, then pull the yarn through the last two loops on your hook (figure 19). You've completed one double crochet stitch. You'll have one loop left on your hook to start your next double crochet.

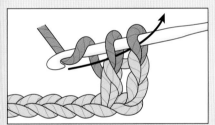

FIGURE 19

5. Bring the yarn over your hook, insert your hook in the next stitch (figure 20), and continue across the row. At the end of the row, turn your work and chain three to make your turning chain (see figure 14).

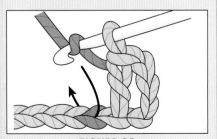

FIGURE 20

HALF DOUBLE CROCHET

The half double crochet (hdc) is used frequently in crochet patterns. It's slightly shorter than a double crochet and taller than a single crochet. To start, make a foundation chain of any number of stitches.

1. Bring the yarn over the hook, locate the third chain stitch from the hook (figure 21), and insert the hook in the chain.

2. Bring the yarn over the hook and catch it with the hook. Pull the hook through the chain. You should have three loops on the hook (figure 22).

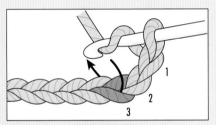

FIGURE 21

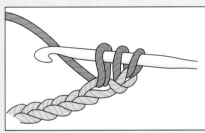

FIGURE 22

3. Bring the yarn over the hook, catch the yarn with the hook, and pull it through the three loops on the hook (figure 23).

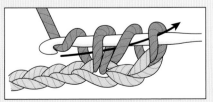

FIGURE 23

4. You will have one loop left on the hook. You've created one half double crochet stitch (figure 24). Yarn over and insert the hook in the next chain and repeat the sequence across the row.

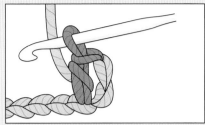

FIGURE 24

TREBLE CROCHET

Treble crochet (tr) is taller than double crochet. It's often used to create an open, lacey fabric.

Start with a foundation chain of any number of stitches.

1. Identify the fifth chain stitch from the hook. Bring the yarn over the hook twice (figure 25).

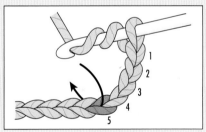

FIGURE 25

2. Insert the hook into the fifth chain. Bring the yarn over the hook, catch the yarn, and pull the hook through the chain. You'll have four loops on the hook (figure 26).

FIGURE 26

3. Bring the yarn over the hook, catch the yarn, and slide the hook through the first two loops (figure 27).

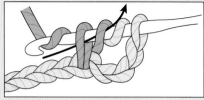

FIGURE 27

4. Yarn over the hook and draw your yarn through the next two loops on the hook (figure 28).

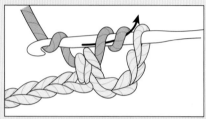

FIGURE 28

5. Yarn over the hook and draw the yarn through the last two loops on your hook (figure 29).

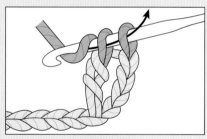

FIGURE 29

6. You will end up with only one loop on your hook. You've completed one treble crochet stitch (figure 30). Yarn over twice and repeat the steps in the next chain stitch.

FIGURE 30

DOUBLE TREBLE

The double treble crochet (dtr) is even taller than a treble crochet. This stitch is best used to create a very loose, openwork fabric.

Make a foundation chain of any number of stitches, then chain five additional stitches for a turning chain.

1. Yarn over the hook three times. Insert the hook in the sixth chain from the hook (figure 31). Yarn over the hook.

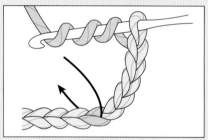

FIGURE 31

2. Gently pull the wrapped hook through the center of the stitch carrying the wrapped yarn through the stitch. You will have five loops on your hook.

3. Yarn over the hook. Draw the yarn through the first two loops on your hook. Repeat this step three more times until you have only one loop on the hook. Start your next dtr by bringing the yarn over three times and inserting the hook in the next chain of the foundation row (figure 32).

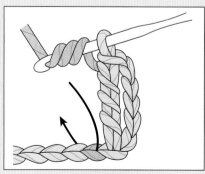

FIGURE 32

4. At the end of the row (figure 33), make five chains to start another row of dtr.

FIGURE 33

SLIP STITCH

The slip stitch (sl st) is a functional stitch with many, many uses. Use this stitch to create a firm finished edge or to join two finished crocheted pieces. You can use a slip stitch to join a new skein of yarn to your crochet project or when you change yarn color. Combine the slip stitch with other stitches to form fancy, complicated-looking stitches. The slip stitch can even be used to create the look of embroidery on crocheted work by simply slip stitching across the surface.

As versatile as it is, the slip stitch is most commonly used to join one end of a foundation chain to the opposite end, forming a ring. The ring then forms the foundation for working pieces in the round (see page 123).

To create a slip stitch, insert the hook into any stitch. Bring the yarn over, catch the yarn, and pull the hook through the stitch and the loop on your hook. (figure 34) This completes one slip stitch. You'll have one loop remaining on the hook.

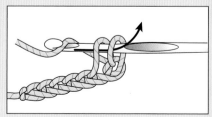

FIGURE 34

SPECIALTY STITCHES

The following stitches are not used in every project but are useful stitches to know and fun to experiment with. Refer to this section if the pattern you're working calls for any of these special stitches.

CLUSTER STITCH

The cluster stitch (no abbreviation) is made up of a number of half-closed stitches (the number of which will be stated in the pattern) worked across an equal number of stitches, and joined at the top. The example shows how to make a cluster with four double crochet stitches.

1. Yarn over, insert the hook into the next stitch, yarn over, draw the yarn through the stitch, yarn over, and draw the yarn through two loops on the hook.

2. Repeat step 1 three times (figure 35).

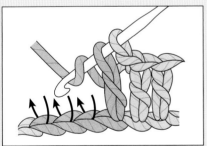

FIGURE 35

3. Yarn over and draw the yarn through all five loops on the hook (figure 36).

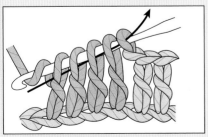

FIGURE 36

FIGURE 37

Figure 37 shows a finished 4-double-crochet cluster stitch.

HAIRPIN LACE

You create hairpin lace on a hairpin fork or loom (also referred to as a hairpin staple). Strips of delicate, airy lace are fashioned by wrapping yarn around two parallel metal prongs, thus forming loops. These loops are then joined with crochet stitches, resulting in strips or strands of fabric.

1. Make a slip knot and slide it over the left upright, positioning the knot so it's centered in the middle. Hold the yarn in front of the loom (figure 38).

2. Cross the yarn over the front of the right upright, wrap it around to the back, and then hold it in place as shown. Insert the hook through the slip-knot and draw the yarn that is in the back of the loom, through the loop to form a loop on your hook (figure 39).

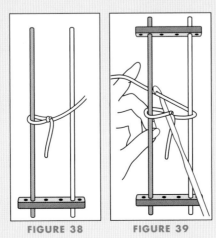

FIGURE 38   **FIGURE 39**

3. Yarn over (figure 40).

4. Draw the yarn through the loop that is on your hook (figure 41).

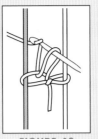 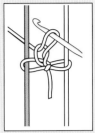

FIGURE 40   **FIGURE 41**

5. Let the loop drop from your hook, then working from the back of the loom, insert the hook back into the dropped loop. Turn the loom clockwise, so that the left and right uprights are in reversed positions (figure 42).

6. When you turned the loom, another loop was formed caused by the yarn wrapping around what is now the right upright. Your hook is now back in front of the loom (figure 43).

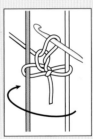 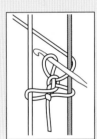

FIGURE 42   **FIGURE 43**

7. Insert your hook under the top strand of the loop on the left upright. Yarn over, and pull the yarn through. You should now have two loops on your hook (figure 44).

8. Yarn over, and draw the yarn through the two loops on your hook (one single crochet will be complete) (figure 45).

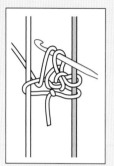 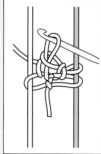

FIGURE 44   **FIGURE 45**

9. Repeat steps 5 through 8. Each time you turn the loom after completing a single crochet between the uprights, a new loop will be formed (figure 46). When your fork is filled, simply remove the wooden bar from the bottom, and slide off all but the last four or five stitches. Replace the bar, and continue working as before until the desired number of loops has been made.

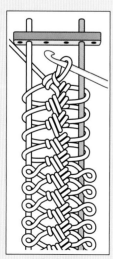

FIGURE 46

PUFF STITCH

As you might guess from its name, the puff stitch (puff st) makes a gently puffed oval shape. The creation of a puff stitch is similar to that of the cluster stitch in that you half-close several stitches worked in the same stitch and then join them at the top to complete the stitch.

1. Yarn over, insert the hook in the next stitch, yarn over, pull the yarn through the stitch, yarn over, and draw the yarn through the two loops on the hook. Two loops remain on the hook (figure 47).

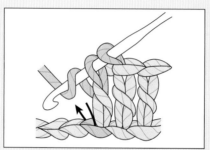

FIGURE 47

2. In the same stitch, repeat step 1 twice. You should have four loops on your hook.

3. Yarn over and draw the yarn through all four loops on the hook (figure 48).

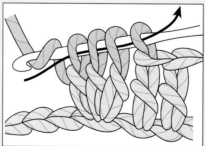

FIGURE 48

See figure 49 for a completed puff stitch.

FIGURE 49

REVERSE SINGLE CROCHET

Just as the name implies, you work this stitch just as you do a regular single crochet—except in reverse. You work the reverse single crochet (reverse sc) from left to right. This stitch is used most frequently for creating a finished edge on your completed work.

1. Work this stitch with the right side of your work facing you. Insert the hook from front to back in the stitch to the right of your hook (figure 50).

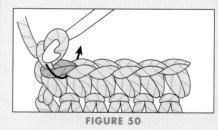

FIGURE 50

2. Bring the yarn over the hook and pull the yarn through the stitch (figure 51.

FIGURE 51

3. Yarn over and bring the yarn through both loops. You've completed one reverse single crochet (figure 52). Continue to work back across the row and fasten off the yarn at the end of the row (see page 124).

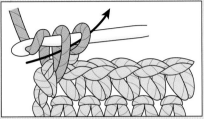

FIGURE 52

CROCHET ANATOMY

You don't have to work crochet stitches in the same way, over and over again. The techniques explained here are used in many different ways: to give different looks to familiar stitches, to change the shape or colors of the piece you're crocheting, or to give you another method for creating crochet. It's useful to carefully examine the basic structure of crocheted fabric. In general, crocheted fabric is composed of stitches and spaces of varying sizes. A completed stitch is composed of the front loop, back loop, and the post. As you work a crochet pattern, you may be directed to work into or around different parts of a stitch or even into the spaces between stitches. These subtle differences in working methods will change the look of the stitch and the finished crochet fabric.

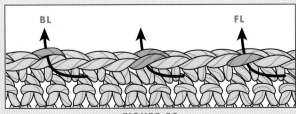

FIGURE 53

STITCH STRUCTURE

BACK AND FRONT LOOPS

As a general rule, a stitch is worked into both top loops of your stitching row; doing so gives you a smooth fabric. Inserting a hook into only the front loop (FL) or back loop (BL) of a stitch creates fabric with a ribbed or ridged look (figure 53). You'll be given specific instructions in your pattern if you're to work into front or back loops.

BACK AND FRONT POST

You can also create raised patterns—resembling ribbing or even intricate cables—with a post stitch. The way you insert your hook around a post—back post (BP) or front post (FP)—determines the look of the stitch. You'll be given specific instructions in your pattern if you need to use this technique to create a stitch (figures 54 and 55).

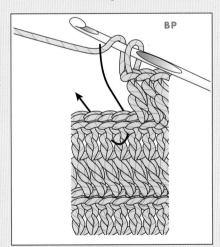

FIGURE 54

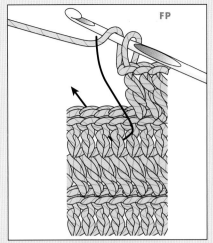

FIGURE 55

CHANGING YARN OR COLOR

Crochet might become boring if you were allowed to use only one color or one type of yarn to create a project. And imagine how difficult it would be if you had to use one—and only one—continuous thread to crochet. It would certainly make crochet a less portable craft.

Should you run out of thread or want to change colors or yarns while you're working, never join a new thread with a knot—it's messy and not an effective method. Whenever possible, it's best to work in a new strand of yarn at the end of a row. So, if you see your yarn diminishing or you think that you may not have enough to finish another row, change your yarn at the end of that row.

Stop just before the last stitch in the row. If you're working in double crochet, work the stitch to the point where you have two loops left on your hook. Drop the old color and wrap the cut end of the new yarn from back to front (figure 56).

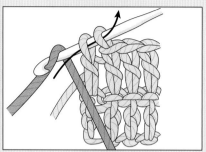

FIGURE 56

Draw the new yarn through the two loops on your hook. Tug on the end of the old yarn to tighten up the stitch. After tightening the stitch, pick up your new color and make your next stitch. If you plan to pick up the first color again right away, read the section on carrying your yarn.

If you don't plan to use the first color again right away, remove your hook from the loop and cut off the first color, leaving a tail to weave in later (see page 124). Insert your hook into the center top of the last double crochet (as shown) down through the center of the stitch (figure 57). Yarn over with the first color's tail; draw the tail up through the stitch. Place the loop of the second color back on the hook, and begin your next row with the second color.

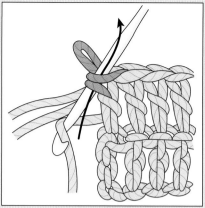

FIGURE 57

CARRYING THE YARN

When a pattern is made up of two or more colors, it would certainly be frustrating to have to change colors every few stitches in the manner described above. You would have a great many yarn ends to weave in when you finished your fabric. However, if you're working on a specific pattern that switches colors often, there's an easier way.

With this method you carry a strand of color across the tops of your stitches in the previous row. It's not unlike working over the end of the yarn when you join a new strand of yarn or color. You lay the unused color of yarn across the tops of the stitches in the previous row and crochet over them (figure 58).

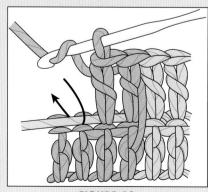

FIGURE 58

To return to the color you have carried, pull the carried color through the last loops of the color you're working to finish the stitch.

SHAPING TECHNIQUES

Working only a rectangle or circle of crochet could be mind numbing and not very useful. There are only so many things you can do with either of those shapes. Simply by adding or subtracting the number of stitches in a row, you can shape the fabric you're creating.

It's very important to count stitches as you increase or decrease according to your pattern (see page 116). Take time to count your stitches, and then count them again!

INCREASING

Increasing stitches simply means adding stitches into a row. Your pattern will tell you when and where to increase (inc). It may be at the beginning, end, or even the middle of the row you're working on. No matter where the increase appears, simply working a given number of stitches into one stitch makes an increase.

Working an increase at the beginning or end of a row is the most common method to add stitches: it gives your fabric a smooth edge. In the example shown, a double crochet increase is worked into the first stitch (figure 59). (Remember: Your turning chain counts as the first stitch!) Figure 60 illustrates a double crochet increase in the middle of a row.

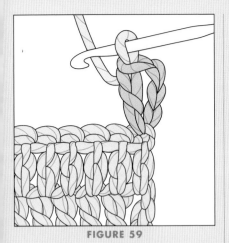

FIGURE 59

FIGURE 60

DECREASING

Decreasing is simply subtracting stitches. A decrease (dec) can be worked at the beginning, end, or middle of a row. Your pattern will tell you precisely where and how to make a decrease. In short, you combine two separate stitches into one stitch. Read your pattern directions carefully so you understand how to work decreases successfully.

For a decrease in double crochet, work a double crochet until you have two loops on your hook. Yarn over your hook and insert it in the next stitch. Yarn over, draw the yarn through the stitch, yarn over and draw the yarn through the first two loops on your hook. Yarn over and draw the yarn through all three loops on your hook.

In the example shown (figure 61), a decrease has been worked in double crochet. If you look at the tops of the stitches, you will see only one stitch crossing the top of two stitch posts.

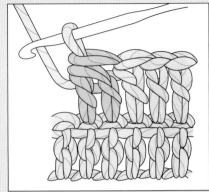

FIGURE 61

WORKING IN THE ROUND

Working crochet in the round is not any more difficult than working back and forth in straight rows. As you work in the round, you will need to increase the number of stitches in each row in order to go around the widening circumference of the circle or length of a tube. Crochet patterns will specify precisely how many stitches you need to use for each round of the pattern.

To crochet in the round, you'll need to create a center ring as a foundation for your stitches. The most common way to do this is to make a chain of any number of stitches, then join the two ends of the chain with a simple slip stitch (see page 118).

1. Create a chain as specified in your pattern. In this example, it's a chain of six (figure 62).

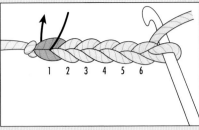

FIGURE 62

2. Insert your hook into the slipknot you made, and bring the yarn over the hook (figure 63).

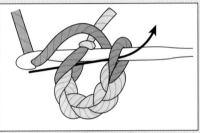

FIGURE 63

3. Pull the yarn through the stitch and through the loop. The foundation ring is completed (figure 64).

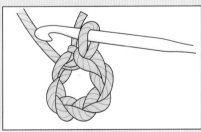

FIGURE 64

After you've made your ring, you can begin to work your first round. The easy part of crocheting in the round is that you'll usually (but not always) make your first stitches into the center of the ring. If you're creating a tube form, you'll work directly into the foundation chain stitches.

It's necessary to mark the beginning of each round with a stitch marker. Otherwise, you won't easily be able to identify where one round begins or ends. The marker can be a commercially made marker, a length of yarn, or even a paper clip.

Working in the round is also one way to begin a Granny Square (see page 96). And how does a circle become a square? Your pattern will tell you how to make the foundation circle into a square by adding chain loops into your row to create the corners of the square.

FINISHING TOUCHES

You've made your very last stitch in a project, but you're not finished yet! As you look at your finished piece, you'll see that edges may be curled or the piece is slightly misshapen. Here are the techniques you'll need to finish off your project.

FASTENING OFF

When you've come to the end of your pattern and made your very last stitch, you'll need to cut your skein of yarn from the crocheted fabric. If you don't fasten the yarn properly, the sight of unraveling stitches will dismay you.

Cut the yarn about six inches from the hook. Draw the end of the yarn through the last loop on your hook (figure 65). Pull the tail of the yarn gently to tighten the loop. This will prevent the accidental unraveling of your stitches.

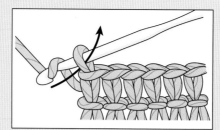

FIGURE 65

WEAVING IN THE END(S)

Thread a large-eyed tapestry needle with the tail of your yarn end. Weave the yarn through three or four stitches (figure 66). To secure the weaving, weave back through the same stitches. Cut the yarn close to—but not up against—the crocheted fabric. Gently pull the fabric, and the yarn end will disappear into the stitches.

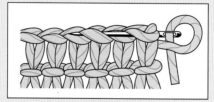

FIGURE 66

Weave in other yarn ends that you have on the wrong side of your fabric in the same way.

PUTTING IT ALL TOGETHER

Crocheted garments—unless they are crocheted in one piece—have to be assembled. There are several different ways to join garment pieces: You can use different sewing stitches or join them with a crochet hook and yarn.

SLIP STITCHING

Using a crochet hook and yarn to join pieces is a neat method. If you work on the wrong side of the piece, a strong seam results. If you work on the right side of a piece, a decorative, embroidered stitch results. If needed, review the slip stitch on page 118.

1. Position two pieces together as directed, with right or wrong sides facing. Take care to be sure that the stitches match across the edge.

2. Work through both pieces using the same size crochet hook you used to crochet the pieces. Insert the hook through the back two loops of the first two stitches. Leave a yarn tail.

3. Yarn over, pull the yarn through. Repeat the stitch in each stitch across the seam (figure 67). Weave in the yarn ends when you have stitched across the seam.

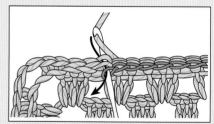

FIGURE 67

DESIGNER BIOS

Hollie Dzama is majoring in Fiber Arts at Concordia University in Montreal, Quebec, Canada. As well as crocheting, she also enjoys painting, sewing toys and clothing, and karaoke. You can see more of Hollie's work at www.holliedzama.com.

Paula Gron lives with her sculptor husband, Jack, and their cat in the beautiful coastal community of Corpus Christi, Texas. Her first craft project—at age eight—was a saddle made out of newspaper and rope, for the porch railing. As an award-winning graphic designer and commercial illustrator, Paula has combined design with her love of crafting. Some of her recent designs are featured in *The New Crochet: 40 Wonderful Wearables* (Lark, 2005). You can find her designs in craft publications and through yarn manufacturers.

Deborah Grossman has been designing accessories since she was a child—from crocheted chokers and hammered-brass earrings in the 1970s, to the recent craze for shrugs and ponchos (with a brief and clandestine foray into doilies). And always hats. Dulcinea Design was established in 2001 and offers the Dulcinea line of handbags, and the Dulce Collection, an ever-changing and expanding line of accessories (www.dulcineadesign.com). Deborah is inspired by her mother, father, brother, her nine-year-old son, and her pretend sister Julie, all of whom are artists.

Don Halstead combines his talents of 25+ years as a graphic designer/artist/web designer and 30+ years designing knitting and crochet patterns into colorful and unique patterns for hats and caps. After looking endless years in retail outlets to no avail for a certain type of cap, Don decided to design and knit/crochet his own. Some 50+ hat designs later, it seemed a logical conclusion to market his patterns. To see more of Don's original hat patterns, visit www.hatternique.com.

Jennifer Hansen lives in Fremont, California, where she is a full-time designer, teacher, and writer. Her innovative work has been featured in various books and magazines including *Vogue Knitting, Interweave Crochet*, and *The Happy Hooker*. She also publishes designs through her company, Stitch Diva Studios. Stitch Diva Studios patterns are available for download, and may also be purchased at yarn stores nationwide. You can visit Stitch Diva Studios online at www.stitchdiva.com to view more of Jennifer's designs.

Jonathan James learned to crochet from a cute woman who snuggled up next to him and held his hands the first time. It never occurred to him that he would grow up to be a hooker. Since then he has consistently made funky hats based on his imagination, not on patterns. Jonathan is a traditional astrologer, a writer, once spent a week teaching poetry in Alaska to schoolchildren, and has just opened a shop in his adopted village of Woodstock, New York. His parents are retired newspaper publishers (Jonathan's father is also a book author and writer), his siblings live in six different states, and he has tried marriage once. Da Vinci has always been his hero. See Jonathan's work at www.woodstockhooker.com.

Kalpna Kapoor lives with her husband and three kids in Santa Clarita, California. Her mother taught her to knit and crochet at a very young age. Her designs have been published in several books including *The New Crochet: 40 Wonderful Wearables* (Lark 2005), and *Fabulous Crocheted Ponchos: New Styles, New Looks, New Yarns* (Lark 2005). Kalpna owns Craft-Creations Knitting Studios in Santa Clarita, and teaches both knitting and crochet workshops. You can visit her website at www.knittingand-crochet.com to view more of her designs as well as a wide selection of fine yarns from around the world.

Gwen Blakley Kinsler is the founder of the Crochet Guild of America, and has been in the forefront of promoting crochet as fashion since 1992. By teaching classes, promoting art exhibits, and more simply by wearing it every day, she has surprised and enlightened countless people about crochet, and is committed to the importance of sharing her passion with anyone interested in learning, especially children. She co-authored *Crocheting—Kids Can Do It* with Jackie Young (Kids Can Press, 2003). Visit www.crochetqueen.com to see more of Gwen's designs.

Dot Matthews learned to crochet when she was 12. Her mom taught her the stitches and how to make a doily, but she didn't learn to read a pattern until she was 19. Dot is retired with two grown sons and nine grandchildren. She has been designing her own patterns since 2004, and enjoys crocheting for family, friends, and charitable events. To see more of Dot's work, visit her blogs http://bythehook.blogdrive.com/, and http://patbythehook.blogdrive.com/.

Marty Miller equates a day without crochet to a day without sunshine. Ever since her grandmother taught her to crochet when she was a young girl, Marty has been designing patterns for herself and others. Her comfortable, unique garments and accessories have been widely published in books and magazines. In addition to teaching crochet classes both locally and nationally, Marty is now the Professional Development Chairperson for the Crochet Guild of America. Her grandmother would be so proud!

Emily North (also known as Em Sixteen) is a writer and guerilla art-maker. When she's not working her day job as a Graphic Designer in NYC, she's drawing, working on digital art projects, and obsessively making things with her hands. She is co-editor of riffRAG.org, a political feminist art magazine, and is sole proprietor of m16handmade.com, her online store for wearable handmade items. View her current projects at www.em16.com.

Lindsay Obermeyer holds an M.F.A. from the University of Washington, an M.A.T. from National-Louis University, and a B.F.A. from the School of the Art Institute of Chicago. Her work has been widely exhibited throughout the United States in venues including Boston's Museum of Fine Arts, the Milwaukee Art Museum, and the Museum of Arts and Design. Lindsay has taught at Northern Illinois University, National-Louis University, and School of the Art Institute of Chicago, among others. She was a contributing writer to *Reinventing Textiles: Gender and Identity*. Visit her website at www.lbostudio.com.

ABBREVIATIONS

alt	alternate
alt lp st	alternate loop stitch
approx	approximately
beg	begin, beginning
BL	back loop
BP	back post
ch	chain
ch-sp	chain space
cont	continue
dc	double crochet
dec	decrease(s/ing)
dtr	double treble crochet
ea	each
FL	front loop
FP	front post
hdc	half double crochet
hk	hook
inc	increase(s/ing)
lp(s)	loop(s)
lp st	loop stitch
oz	ounce(s)
prev	previous
puff st	puff stitch
rem	remaining
rep	repeat
reverse sc	reverse single crochet
RS	right side
rnd(s)	round(s)
sc	single crochet
sk	skip
sl st	slip stitch
sp	space(s)
st(s)	stitch(es)
tch	turning chain
tog	together
tr	treble crochet
WS	wrong side
yo	yarn over

CROCHET HOOK SIZES

Continental	U.S.
2.25 mm	B-1
2.75 mm	C-2
3.25 mm	D-3
3.5 mm	E-4
3.75 mm	F-5
4 mm	G-6
4.5 mm	7
5 mm	H-8
5.5 mm	I-9
6 mm	J-10
6.5 mm	K-10 1/2
8 mm	L-11
9 mm	M/N-13
10 mm	N/P-15
15 mm	P/Q
16 mm	Q
19 mm	S

*Letter or number may vary by manufacturer. For accurate and consistent sizing, rely on the millimeter (mm) size.

ACKNOWLEDGMENTS

Thank you to the following people for their vital contributions to this book:

Fiber art and craft artist Sharon Mann, for providing the lovely crocheted brooch shown on the Town & Country Felted Bucket. You can see more of her work at www.sharonmanndesigns.com.

Wonderfully meticulous Karen Manthey for her methodical ways, ensuring that each stitch is in its proper place.

Fellow Lark editor Terry Taylor, for his vast and invaluable literary and pictorial donations.

Hat aficionado Archie Burkel, for her gracious permission to reprint the inspirational hat quotes found at the front of this book. To learn which hat style best flatters your face and body shape, and other hat tips and tidbits, or to find out how to start "The Hat Ladies" in your town, visit www.hat-ladies.org.

And finally, to all the talented crochet designers, for sharing their visions that are the essence of this book.

METRIC CONVERSION CHART

Inches	Centimeters
1/8	3 mm
1/4	6 mm
3/8	9 mm
1/2	1.3
5/8	1.6
3/4	1.9
7/8	2.2
1	2.5
1 1/4	3.1
1 1/2	3.8
1 3/4	4.4
2	5
2 1/2	6.25
3	7.5
3 1/2	8.8
4	10
4 1/2	11.3
5	12.5
5 1/2	13.8
6	15
7	17.5
8	20
9	22.5
10	25
11	27.5
12	30
1 ft	30

INDEX